Facts and Photos for Readers of All Ages

UNION
SOLDIERS

in the American Civil War

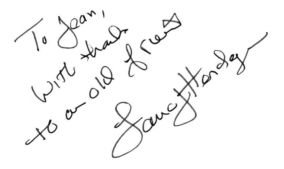

Lance J. Herdegen

Savas Beatie
California

Library of Congress Cataloging-in-Publication Data

Names: Herdegen, Lance J., author.
Title: Union Soldiers in the American Civil War: Facts and Photos for Readers of All Ages / by Lance J. Herdegen.
Description: First edition. | El Dorado Hills, California : Savas Beatie LLC, 2018. | Includes bibliographical references and index.
Identifiers: LCCN 2018043002| ISBN 9781611213393 (pbk : alk. paper) | ISBN 9781611213409 (ebk)
Subjects: LCSH: Soldiers--United States--History--19th century. | United States--History--Civil War, 1861-1865. | United States. Army--History--Civil War, 1861-1865. | United States. Army--Military life--History--19th century.
Classification: LCC E607 .H47 2017 | DDC 973.7/41--dc23
LC record available at https://lccn.loc.gov/2017043002

ISBN (print): 978-1-61121-339-3 / ISBN (ebook): 978-1-61121-340-9

First Edition, First Printing

SB

Savas Beatie LLC
989 Governor Drive, Suite 102
El Dorado Hills, CA 95762

MIX
Paper from responsible sources
FSC
www.fsc.org   FSC® C011935

Phone: 916-941-6896 / (web) www.savasbeatie.com / (E-mail) sales@savasbeatie.com

Savas Beatie titles are available at special discounts for bulk purchases in the United States by corporations, institutions, and other organizations. For more details, please contact Savas Beatie, P.O. Box 4527, El Dorado Hills, CA 95762, or you may e-mail us at sales@savasbeatie.com, or visit our website at www.savasbeatie.com for additional information.

Proudly published, printed, and warehoused in the United States of America.

For Shirley Ann
Bonnie, Lisa, Jill, Jennifer and Nicole

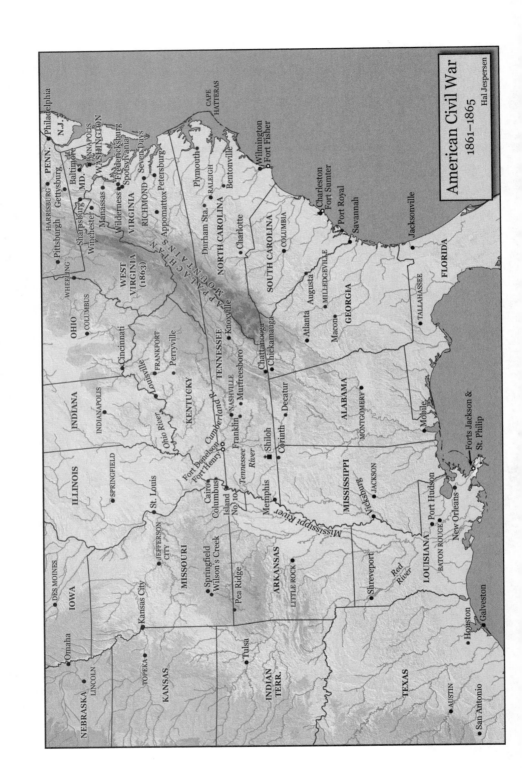

American Civil War
1861–1865
Hal Jespersen

Table of Contents

Table of Contents (continued)

Introduction

My lifelong interest in the Union soldier began when I was 12, when my father brought home a musket and sword he found while helping a friend clean out a shed. The rifled-musket was an 1861 Colt Special Model, dated 1864. It was still at full-length with three bands, but—obviously war surplus—the rifling in the barrel had been partially ground away to make a shotgun for commercial trade.

The weapon completely fascinated me. Being a true son of the Badger state, I had to learn to shoot it. That led me to a local muzzle-loading rifle club, and then—with a better ordnance—to the marksmanship competitions with Civil War small arms in the North-South Skirmish Association.

The journey, and my growing fascination with the Civil War, also raised lingering questions about the Union soldier who has come to us as simply "Billy Yank." From an early age I wondered, "Why did so many young men flock to the flag in 1861?" "What did he eat and how did he get his food?" "What additional equipment did he carry?" "What did he look like?" "Was he tall?" "How old were Yankee soldiers?" "What were his chances of being killed or wounded in battle?" I was also curious about their general views on the Union itself, and, of course, the institution of slavery.

Reading books raised even more questions: "What is a company, or a regiment, brigade, division, or corps?" I didn't know, and most books just assumed that I did. "What did they do in the winter?" "What happened to men when they were wounded?" The answers, as I eventually learned, could be found in other sources—but they were not always quickly at hand, and in some cases, they were not all that easy to find.

Later, I found many of the answers to my own questions, and, of course scores of others, while serving as the Director of The Institute for Civil War

Studies at what is now Carroll University in Wisconsin. Other information was researched by the good folks at the Civil War Museum of the Upper Middle West at Kenosha, Wisconsin, a place that should be on the must-visit list of anyone interested in the 1861-65 period. The museum tells a unique and insightful story not always found in other such facilities.

Union Soldiers in the American Civil War (soon to be accompanied by a similar book titled *Confederate Soldiers in the American Civil War*, by Mark Hughes) is written in the present tense for more immediacy, and is intended as a quick resource—an easy, informative, and engaging reading experience. This book was written for anyone who wants to know more about the Civil War in general, and Union soldiers and sailors in particular.

I am sure you will find—as I do—that the soldiers who fought for the Union so long ago were an interesting and varied lot. I am also sure you will come to value your acquaintance with these boys who left home only to be caught up in a war that forever changed them and their beloved nation.

Lance J. Herdegen
Town of Spring Prairie
Walworth County, Wisconsin

Acknowledgments

The writing and research needed to prepare a book appears to be the work of one person. In fact, it is the work of many. Countless hands—often stretching back over a lifetime—stir the kettle and influence the final pages. To the following, in no special order, I offer thanks: Daniel Netteshiem, Gary Van Kauwenberg, Paul Johnson, Phil Spaugy, Kim J. Heltemes, Andy Ackeret, Donna Agnelly, with a special nod to my colleagues at The Civil War Museum of the Upper Middle West, Dan Joyce, Gina Radandt, Ruth Joyce, and Doug Dammann. Many others also helped—too many to name them all here. Know that I appreciate all everyone has done to make this book possible.

A special thanks and a lifting of a glass of Apple Jack for my friend, editor, and publisher Theodore P. Savas. His efforts, along with the good folks at Savas Beatie, will have a lasting impact on Civil War scholarship for their outstanding books on the 1861-65 era.

And somewhere, across the dark river in a quiet camp where the pet dog of Captain Werner von Bachelle still frolics, I am sure James Patrick Sullivan, "Mickey, of Company K," is smiling.

He is Called Billy Yank

The common Union soldier in the American Civil War is known by many names. The Confederates across the lines call him a "Bluebelly" (for the color of his uniform) or a "Mudsill" (a reference to society's lower classes), and even a "Lincolnite" (for his politics), but the name carried down through the decades is simply "Billy Yank."

Statistics kept in 1861 to 1865 give us a composite picture of the typical Union soldier. He is generally about 25 years old, but many Union soldiers are 18 or slightly older. A few are as old as 60. Most are born in America, but many are foreign born. Germany furnished 175,000 men to the war effort, Ireland 150,000, and England 50,000. Billy Yank stands a bit above 5-foot-8, but soldiers from a few states, including Indiana and Iowa, are slightly

This unidentified sergeant of the 28th Wisconsin Infantry poses in Milwaukee before his regiment is sent to the front in 1862. He displays his non-commissioned officer belts and sword. *Author's Collection*

An unidentified sergeant of an Ohio regiment poses in a studio, circa 1863.
Author's Collection

taller. Of one million men recorded, more than 3,613 are taller than 6-ft., 3 inches. Several stand taller than 7 feet. The average solder weighs 143 ½ pounds, and more than half have dark (black or brown) hair. One percent has gray hair. Almost three-fourths of the soldiers have blue or grey eyes.

More than three-quarters of the soldiers are farmers or mechanics, with just three percent in professional trades. Tall men sometimes prove to be poor material for a toilsome campaign. As one officer would later write at the end of a long hard march, the "ponies"—the short fellows who trudged along at the tail of the company—are generally all still there.

This is part of the story of Billy Yank: who he is, how he got caught up in the Civil War, and how he lives as a soldier.

The Coming Storm

By the 1850s, the North is caught up in an industrial revolution that is changing daily lives while the South prospers agriculturally. In both sections, more Americans value literacy and education. About 90 percent of adults can read and write at a third grade level. Almost three-fourths of children in the North between the ages of 5 and 19 attend school for about six months of the year.

Separated by economic systems of industry and agriculture, the two sections drift apart through the years over the issues of slavery and sectionalism. The turning point arrives with the 1860 election of Republican Abraham Lincoln of Illinois as president. South Carolina is the first to leave the Union, followed by Florida, Alabama, Georgia, Louisiana, and Texas. Delegates from the seceded states meet in mid-February of 1861 at Montgomery, Alabama, to work on a provisional constitution establishing the Confederate States of America. The announcement sets off a wave of celebrations across the South, shrill wild yells that would soon echo on 100 battlefields. In early April 1861 attention turns to Charleston, South Carolina, where Maj. Robert Anderson holds Fort Sumter in the harbor. Anderson refuses Confederate demands for the fort surrender. At dawn on April 12, 1861, Confederate batteries open fire on Fort Sumter.

The attack prompts President Abraham Lincoln to call for 75,000 volunteers to put down the rebellion. The call and the firing on Sumter rouse a wave of patriotism in the North. A civil war, so long threatened, is underway.

After the Southern states secede, one of Lincoln's rivals in the presidential election, Senator Stephen A. Douglas of Illinois, travels South urging a peaceful reunion. After Fort Sumter, however, Douglas warns in a speech at Chicago,

A student reads with her teacher (below), while children at a school in Iowa pose with their teachers (left). *Author's Collection*

"There can be no neutrals in this war, only patriots or traitors." The statement is greeted with loud cheers.

A speaker at one of the war rallies in the Upper Middle West proclaimed, "If our forefathers fought for seven dreadful years to give us this Government, we should be willing to fight seven times seven to prevent its overthrow."

Everywhere across the Northern states, young men by the tens of thousands gathered to volunteer and defend the American Union. All of are excited about the new experiences they would share. None of them understand what they are about to endure.

A Concise Timeline of the American Civil War

1860

November 6: Abraham Lincoln is elected as the 16th president of the United States.

December 17: Secession Convention meets in Columbia, South Carolina.

December 20: South Carolina secedes from the Union.

1861

January: Mississippi, Florida, Alabama, Georgia, Louisiana, and Texas secede from the Union.

February 8-9: Confederacy forms at Montgomery, Alabama.

February 18: Jefferson Davis is appointed president of the Confederate States of America.

March 4: Abraham Lincoln is inaugurated.

April 12: Southern forces fire on Fort Sumter at Charleston, South Carolina.

April 15: Lincoln issues call for 75,000 volunteers to stop the rebellion.

June 3: Skirmish near Philippi western Virginia.

June 10: Battle of Big Bethel, the first land battle of the war in Virginia.

July 21: First Battle of Bull Run (Manassas), in Virginia.

August 10: Battle of Wilson's Creek, in Missouri.

August 28-29: Fort Hatteras in North Carolina falls to Union naval forces.

September 20: Lexington, Missouri, falls to Confederate forces.

October 21: Battle of Ball's Bluff, in Virginia, where many Union men are shot or drown in the cold waters of the Potomac River.

1862

January 19: Battle of Mill Springs, in Kentucky.

February 6: Surrender of Fort Henry, in Tennessee.

February 8: Battle of Roanoke Island, North Carolina.

February 16: Surrender of Fort Donelson, in Tennessee.

March 7-8: Battle of Pea Ridge or Elkhorn Tavern, Arkansas.

March 9: The ironclads USS *Monitor* and CSS *Virginia* fight a history-making battle to a draw at Hampton Roads, Virginia.

April 6-7: Battle of Shiloh (Pittsburg Landing) in Tennessee.

April 24-25: Fall of New Orleans to a Union fleet of gunships.

May 25: First Battle of Winchester, in Virginia.

May 31-June 1: Battle of Seven Pines near Richmond, Virginia.

June 6: Battle of Memphis, Tennessee.

June 25-July 1: Seven Days' Battle before Richmond.

August 28-30: Second Battle of Bull Run (Manassas) in Virginia.

September 17: Battle of Antietam (Sharpsburg) in Maryland.

December 13: Battle of Fredericksburg, Virginia.

December 31-January 3, 1863: Battle of Stones River (Murfreesboro) in Tennessee.

1863

January 1: Emancipation Proclamation takes effect.

March 3: The drafting of soldiers into military service begins in the North.

May 1-4: Battle of Chancellorsville, Virginia.

May 10: Confederate General Thomas "Stonewall" Jackson dies of wounds from friendly fire.

May 18: Siege of Vicksburg, Mississippi, begins.

June 9: Gettysburg campaign opens.

June 9: Battle of Brandy Station, Virginia.

June 14-15: Second Battle of Winchester, Virginia.

July 1-3: Battle of Gettysburg, Pennsylvania.

July 4: Vicksburg, Mississippi, surrenders to Maj. Gen. Ulysses S. Grant.

July 13: Draft Riots begin in New York City.

July 13-14: The Gettysburg campaign ends near Falling Waters, Maryland.

July 18: Second assault on Battery Wagner, South Carolina.

August 21: Sacking of Lawrence, Kansas.

September 9: Chattanooga, Tennessee, is occupied.

September 19-20: Battle of Chickamauga, Georgia.

September–November 1863: Siege of Chattanooga, Tennessee.

October 9-22: Bristoe Station campaign in Virginia.

November 19: Abraham Lincoln gives a brief speech at Gettysburg, Pennsylvania.

November 24-25: Battles of Lookout Mountain and Missionary Ridge.

November 26-December 1: Mine Run campaign in Virginia.

November 27 to December 3: Siege of Knoxville, Tennessee.

1864

February 9: Escape from Libby Prison in Richmond.

February 27, 1864: Andersonville prison camp is opened in Georgia.

February 14-20: Union forces capture Meridian, Mississippi.

February 17: The submersible CSS *H.L. Hunley* sinks the USS *Houstonic* outside of Charleston, South Carolina, in the first successful submarine attack in history.

March 3: Ulysses S. Grant assumes command of all Union armies in the field.

March 10: Red River campaign begins in Louisiana.

April 8: Battle of Sabine Crossroads or Mansfield, in Louisiana.

April 9: Battle of Pleasant Hill, in Louisiana.

April 12: Capture of Fort Pillow, in Tennessee

May 4-5: Battle of the Wilderness in Virginia.

May 7: Opening of the Atlanta campaign in Georgia.

May 8-21: Battles around Spotsylvania Court House in Virginia.

May 11: Battle of Yellow Tavern in Virginia, and mortal wounding of Confederate cavalry commander Maj. Gen. James E. B. Stuart.

May 14-15: Battle of Resaca, in Georgia.

June 1-3: Battle of Cold Harbor, in Virginia.

June 8: Abraham Lincoln is nominated for a second term as president.

June 10: The Battle of Brice's Crossroads, Mississippi.

June 15-18: The assault on Petersburg, Virginia.

June 19: USS *Kearsarge* sinks the Confederate raider CSS *Alabama* near Cherbourg, France.

June 27: Battle of Kennesaw Mountain, in Georgia.

July 11-12: Attack on the defenses of Washington, D.C.

July 14-15: Battles near Tupelo, Mississippi.

July 20: Battle of Peachtree Creek, Georgia, near Atlanta, Georgia.

July 22: Battle of Atlanta, in Georgia

July 30: Battle of the Crater near Petersburg, Virginia.

August 5: Mobile Bay in Alabama captured by Union forces.

August 18-19: Battles on the Weldon Railroad near Petersburg, Virginia.

August 25: Battle of Ream's Station, near Petersburg, Virginia

August 31 - September 1, 1864: Battle of Jonesborough, in Georgia.

September 2: Fall of Atlanta, Georgia

September 19: Third Battle of Winchester, in Virginia.

September 22: Battle of Fisher's Hill, in Virginia.

September 29-30: Battle of Fort Harrison near Richmond, in Virginia

October 19: Battle of Cedar Creek, in Virginia.

November 8: Lincoln is reelected president of the United States.

November 16: General Sherman's Army of Georgia begins the "March to the Sea."

November 30: Battle of Franklin, in Tennessee.

December 10: Sherman's Army arrives at Savannah, Georgia, completing the "March to the Sea."

December 15-16: Battle of Nashville, in Tennessee.

1865

January 15: Capture of Fort Fisher, in North Carolina.

February 1: Sherman's Army leaves Savannah to march through the Carolinas.

February 17: Columbia, South Carolina, is captured.

February 22, 1865: Wilmington, North Carolina, falls to Union troops.

March 4: Lincoln inaugurated for his second term as president.

March 11: Sherman's army occupies Fayetteville, North Carolina.

March 16 and 19-21: Battles of Averasboro and Bentonville, in North Carolina.

March 25: Attack on Fort Stedman at Petersburg, in Virginia.

April 1: Battle of Five Forks, in Virginia.

April 3: Union troops occupy Richmond and Petersburg, Virginia.

April 6: Battle of Sailor's Creek, in Virginia.

April 9: Surrender at Appomattox Court House, Virginia.

April 12: Confederate Army of Northern Virginia is formally disbanded.

April 14: Lincoln is assassinated by actor John Wilkes Booth.

April 14: Fort Sumter in South Carolina is reoccupied by Union troops.

April 26: The Confederate Army of the Tennessee surrenders near Durham, North Carolina.

May 4: General Richard Taylor surrenders Confederate forces in the Department of Alabama, Mississippi and East Louisiana.

May 10: Confederate President Jefferson Davis is captured near Irwinville, Georgia.

May 12: The final battle of the Civil War, a Confederate victory, takes place at Palmito Ranch, Texas.

May 23: Grand Review of the Army of the Potomac in Washington, D.C.

May 24: Grand Review of General Sherman's army in Washington, D.C.

May 26: Confederate Army of the Trans-Mississippi surrenders and the American Civil War officially ends.

June 23: The last major Confederate force to surrender is led by Cherokee General Stand Watie, who stands down with his Indian soldiers.

November 6: The raider CSS *Shenandoah* surrenders at Liverpool, England.

Did You Know?
Interesting Facts about Soldier Life

Among the more popular reading forms before and during the Civil War are such **weekly newspapers** as *Frank Leslie's Illustrated Weekly*, *Harper's Weekly*, and the *Illustrated London News*. These papers feature news pages filled with elaborate engravings. While correspondents use words to report the latest war news, a group of artists travel with them to make drawings of newsworthy events and personalities. These artists are called "Specials," and for the first time add a visual record of a war.

The Union has a decided **river advantage**. For example, the Mississippi, Tennessee, and Cumberland rivers in the Western Theater (the land west of the Appalachian Mountains and east of the Mississippi River) flows mostly north to south, aiding Federal forces moving into the heart of the Confederacy. Union troops would fight their way down the Mississippi River in a series of combined naval and land operations for nearly 18 months. The fall of Vicksburg, a major Southern stronghold in Mississippi, in July 1863 puts control of the great river into Union hands and all but dooms the Confederacy.

By June 1862, the **U.S. Quartermaster's Department** has purchased $3.4 million worth of boots and shoes, $3 million of trousers and $1.4 million of blankets. The large purchases are usually fair, but others are tainted by graft and fraud. The quality of items, depending on the manufacturer, range from excellent to shoddy. The soles of shoes worn by some soldiers fall apart when they get wet because they are made of thin leather and paper, and hats dissolve in rain. Salt beef is often rancid—green and uneatable.

Steamships docked at the wharf at Vicksburg, Mississippi. *LOC*

Monthly pay for officers ranges from $270 for a lieutenant general and $220 for a major general to $45 for a second lieutenant of infantry or artillery. In ranks, a sergeant-major makes $21 and a private just $13.

The **last living Union veteran** of the Civil War is reported to be Albert Woolson, who dies in Duluth, Minnesota, on August 2, 1956 at the age of 109. He was only 17 when detailed to the Heavy Artillery's drum corps and serves for less than a year doing occupation duty in the South. The last man who sees combat was 37th New York's James Hard (1843-1953), who fights at First Bull Run, Antietam, and Chancellorsville, and even meets President Abraham Lincoln.

Rivers are the main transportation arteries in the Western Theater. Many river steamers convert to **hospital ships**, staffed with doctors and nurses, to accommodate wounded or sick soldiers. The more elaborate Union hospital ships have large water towers that provide hot and cold water for bathing, special drinking faucets on the decks, and even protection from fire.

The Union hospital ship *Nashville* on the Mississippi River. LOC

By 1864, General U.S. Grant's army requires 4,000 **heavy wagons** to haul its gear while General William Tecumseh Sherman's army group (three armies working together) includes 5,180 wagons, 860 ambulances, 28,300 horses, and 32,600 mules.

Union Army wagons entering Petersburg, Virginia, April 1865. LOC

An unidentified Union officer with profile bust pin of an unidentified man and wearing a Hardee hat. *LOC*

The raising of the volunteer regiments brings wagon loads of food, clothing, medical supplies, and money from individual citizens for Union soldiers. The mostly uncoordinated effort with no military policy on how to deal with it leaves shipping areas piled with rotting foodstuffs and undelivered supplies. The **U.S. Sanitary Commission** is organized to coordinate benevolent activities as well as the improvement of cleanliness in the sprawling soldier camps.

Union telegrapher workers in the field. *Author's Collection*

Watching soldiers always stare in wonder as men of the **U.S. Telegraph Service** loop miles of copper wire that help make large-scale troop movements possible in 1861-1865. It is an innovative and dangerous job that claims a 10 percent casualty rate among field operators. Most of the skilled telegraphers are civilians employed by the Quartermaster Department.

Two of the most elite units in the Union Army are the 1st and 2nd Regiments of **U.S. Sharpshooters** recruited by Colonel Hiram Berdan. Outfitted in dark green uniforms with blackened buttons and skilled in marksmanship, the special companies are part of the Army of the Potomac. The only men accepted are those who can, "when firing at rest, at two hundred yards, put ten consecutive shots in a target, the average distance not to exceed five inches from the center of the bull's eye."

The public thirst for information and the latest war news leads to expanded newspaper coverage and increasing use of graphic images of battlefield action supplied by artist reporters in such publications as *Harper's Weekly* and others. The growing use of bylines on stories also shifts attention away from editors to the reporters themselves—the self-styled **"Bohemian Brigade."** It comes at a time when newspapers are undergoing a revolution from political and editorial sheets to real newspapers carrying the latest happenings.

New York Herald reporters—part of the "Bohemian Brigade." *Author's Collection*

Winter usually brings about a pause in active campaigning because it is much harder to move and feed the armies in the cold weather. The soldiers generally create permanent camps and constructed shelters there. The layout of infantry, cavalry, and artillery camps is prescribed in regulations. The log huts include fireplaces with mud chimneys and a floor of boards. The ground is usually dug out before being floored so a soldier inside the structure—called a **"shebang"**—can stand erect. Wooden bunks are also added.

One necessary component of life in camp is the **Adams Express Company**, which sets up offices in each camp. The company quickly gains a reputation for good service. It is used to distribute packages of food, clothing, and other items sent from home as well as items shipped back to the home states by soldiers. One of the largest boxes weighs nearly 400 pounds and is sent to 20 members of the 6th Wisconsin Artillery.

Called "bread bags" or "war bags," the **haversack** is indispensable to the common soldier. It is usually a bag made of canvas painted black with an inner removable bag of unpainted cotton that can be washed. The haversack is used to carry coffee, salt pork, and hardtack while on campaign. It sometimes also stores a soldier's pipe, matches, and a mess kit.

A **Union battery** also includes a battery wagon, mobile forge, and extra caissons. The battery wagon carries items for the maintenance of the gun ranging from grease and oil to paint and tools, an extra wheel, spokes, 200 pounds of spare harness, and a grindstone. Under ideal conditions, a battery employs 84 draft horses with another two dozen horses used as spares and as riders. The regulation gun crew requires nine men.

The adoption of identifying **corps badges** by Federal forces in 1863 becomes a popular effort to boost unit pride and identification. The woolen patches have different shapes and colors to identify different units. The idea for an identifying badge is credited to Union General Philip Kearny, and the badge system is made army-wide by General Joseph Hooker. Soldiers wear the badges on their hats and on the fronts of their coats. Ornamental enameled versions in gold or silver can be purchased from such firms as Tiffany of New York.

Many Democrats and social and political conservatives are critical of change, oppose the draft, and blame abolitionists for the war. They feel Republican President Abraham Lincoln is a tyrant destroying American values with his despotic and arbitrary actions. Republican opponents call them **"Copperheads"** after the poisonous snake that strikes, and inflate claims of their numbers and plans for their own partisan political gain. Cop- perheadism peaks in early 1863 and fades after Federal victories at Gettysburg and Vicksburg that July.

These 20-pounder Parrott Rifles belong to the 1st New York Battery, photographed here on the Virginia peninsula in 1862. *LOC*

An unidentified Union soldier sports a VI Corps badge. *LOC*

The wife of Louis Pfieff of the 3rd Illinois Infantry goes to Tennessee following the battle of Shiloh, in April 1862, to recover her husband's body. When Louis left home, the family dog went with him. Mrs. Pfieff spent part of day visiting burial sites around the battlefield without success. She was about to give up when the family dog runs toward her. She follows the animal to a solitary grave. The **faithful pet** had been keeping vigil by the grave for 12 days since his master's death, leaving only to search out food.

An estimated 470,851,079 **paper cartridges** are produced by the U.S. Ordnance Department in 1861-65. The cartridge uses a bullet with three grooves with a cavity in the base consisting of a perfect cone. The bullet is .5775

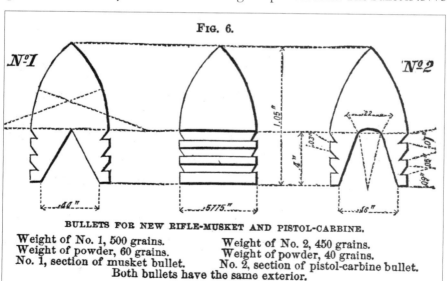

FIG. 6.

N.º1   'N.º 2

BULLETS FOR NEW RIFLE-MUSKET AND PISTOL-CARBINE.

Weight of No. 1, 500 grains.   Weight of No. 2, 450 grains.
Weight of powder, 60 grains.   Weight of powder, 40 grains.
No. 1, section of musket bullet.   No. 2, section of pistol-carbine bullet.
        Both bullets have the same exterior.

inches in diameter, weighs 500 grains (about 1.1 ounce), and is fired with 60 grains of musket powder. A lubricant of one part beeswax and three parts tallow is used in the barrel.

Union Naval Officer Charles Ellet, Jr.'s decision to add a large iron ram to river steamers turns these craft into what becomes known as the **Ellet Ram Fleet**. The rams do not have cannons, but rely on speed to crash into enemy vessels and sink them. The rams play a key role in opening the Tennessee River at Memphis in June 1862, but Ellet is killed in the engagement.

The **USS *Michigan***, built in 1842, is a Federal gunboat launched under an 1818 Treaty allowing the United States to maintain one war vessel on the Great Lakes. During the Civil War, the *Michigan* patrols waterways between the US and Canada and transports and guards Confederate prisoners of war held on Johnson's Island in Lake Erie near Sandusky, Ohio. The *Michigan* is finally retired in 1923. Her guns are never fired in combat.

Echoes from the Union's Fiery Trial

"One method of sustaining commercial relations was to build a raft a foot or so square . . . fix a mast with a news paper for a sail, load the raft with tobacco, and so set the sail that the wind would carry the raft across the river. The recipient would reciprocate in coffee and it was quite common, on asking a man where he got his tobacco, to receive the reply, 'I had a ship come in.'"

— Edward B. Tobie of the 1st Maine Cavalry

"A swift horse, a good pair of spurs, and a sharp saber are the chief weapons of a trooper. Pistols and carbines are but incidentals."

— James H. Stevenson of the 1st New York Cavalry

"Uncle Sam furnishes such good stuff. It is hard tax (tack) and bacon. Take the hard tax and break them up and you will find some very nice bugs to boil up in soup…. That is where we cheat the government. We get livestock that is counted as nothing."

— Unknown Michigan soldier

Union cavalry commander Gen. Judson Kilpatrick, an advocate of the "sharp saber." LOC

A rather "rough" looking Union man from the Iron Brigade. LOC

"Wash the scalp thoroughly every morning. Let the whole beard grow. This protects the lungs against dust and the threat against winds and cold in winter. In the summer, it induces a greater perspiration of the skin—hence, greater coolness of the parts outside, while the throat is less feverish and dry."

— *The Soldier's Health Companion*

"The slave-hunters appear to be particularly busy in Wisconsin. At the last accounts they were in pursuit of a female, about 24 years of age, nearly white, and beautiful, who has been residing for some time in Kenosha. But the matter somehow got out, and when the kidnappers arrived in that city, the bird had flown, having taken the express train for Canada several hours previous to their arrival."

— *Sabbath Recorder*, 1854

"I will send you my lovely face and next time I get it taken it will be in the old style long hair and beard. This is a rough picture but perhaps it is more like me than any other for I am a rough man."

— Letter, Oliver Fletcher, Company K, 6th Wisconsin, May 28, 1862

"Oh I tell you there is more beaux here than you could shake a stick at in a year. Tell Abby Rodgers if she wants to get married she better come out here for she would not be here a week before she would have a dozen offers."

— Mary Lanphear of Minnesota to her sister

"O, Mary, it is sad to look now at our shattered band of devoted men. Only four field officers in the brigade have escaped and I am one of them."

— Rufus Dawes, letter to Mary Gates, July 4, 1863, Gettysburg, Pennsylvania

Mary Beman Gates of Marietta, Ohio, in a photo taken in 1862. *Author's Collection*

"I can tell you most of the boys are willing to acknowledge having seen enough of the elephant to distinguish his ears at least and think if we have to serve out our three years he will be visible without the aid of an opera glass."

— Lewis Spotts, 84th Indiana, November 15, 1862

The day in camp began at 5 a.m. and continued until 9:15 p.m. "Then the poor greenhorn patriot, tired as an ox after a day's hard logging was at liberty to lay down on the soft side of a board and dream, if he slept at all, of glory and the grave."

— Pvt. James Sullivan, 6th Wisconsin Infantry

"Sgt. Benjamin Franklin Brown of the 87th Indiana saw Confederates "as thick as I ever saw pigeons on a newly sown corn field."

— *Rochester* (Indiana) *Chronicle*, October 15, 1863

"There are [in Washington] whole platoons of liquor stores, and then more liquor stores, and traveling on you just begin to come to the liquor stores. . . . Whiskey is contraband. It is not permitted to be taken over the river to the camps. . . . As for the army it gets its whiskey in a modest and demure way. Cans, labeled 'Oysters,' and 'Pickles' and "preserved meats," are very popular with the army."

— Unknown Union soldier

Teamster Daniel Bruce, 84th Indiana, awoke to find frozen trousers "so that I could not get them on for some time, working them and rubbing them. Coat froze stiff. I shivered like a dog." The next night, "I could sleep but little

Three unidentified Union soldiers playing cards and drinking, likely taken early in the war before the real horrors of combat came calling. *Author's Collection*

on account of the cold I thought sometimes I had frozen my feet. I never felt as cold as I did this date.

— *Rochester* (Indiana) *Chronicle*, October 22, 1863

"Tell Mother I don't forget what she told me about gamboling [sic] and drinking. I think I shall stand it very well, Father."

— Drummer Boy Charles A. Carter, 17th Wisconsin, Letter, March 27, 1863. He died at Marietta, Georgia, September 17, 1864

"I had often wondered in reading of heavy battles, why more men were not killed as the bullets flew so thick. I am still at a loss to know the reason. The balls flew thick all around us and few were killed, comparatively speaking. I received a slight tap with a musket ball upon the thigh but it was so far spent that it done me no particular injury."

— Pvt. Frederick Kiner, 14th Indiana, on Fort Donelson, February 1862

"At the foremost picket-posts, in the rifle-pits, and in the advance parallels, at any hour of the day or the night, you can listen to the mysterious yet intellectual click of the telegraph instrument."

—Col. Anson Stager, U.S. Military Telegraph

"I have often (heard) men say that they would night fight beside a negro soldier, but on the 15th the whites and blacks charged together and they fell as well as we did... I have seen a great (many) fighting for our country. Then why should they not be free."

— A private in the 89th Illinois Infantry

"Not being able to earn to drill, and too dirty to appear on inspection, he is sent to the cook house to get him out of ranks. We were not sorry when the cook house was abolished."

— An anonymous New York private

"The earth seemed crashing into a thousand atoms. The sky... seemed boiling with smoke and flame. And the horrid shrieking shot, and bursting shells, then the shouting of commanders and cheer of men, mingled with the sputter of muskets and the roar of batteries, made the world about us seem like a very hell."

— An 18-year-old private describing his first battle

"His knapsack lay at his feet, his musket was propped against a post... He did not hear us until we were close upon him, and even after he turned, my mother hesitated, so thin, so hollow eyed, so changed was he... I could not relate him to the father I had heard so much about. To me he was only a strange man with big eyes and care worn face. I did not recognize in him anything I had ever known."

— Hamlin Garland, West Salem, Wisconsin, on the return of his father

Organization of the Union Armies

Union armies are the land forces that fight the Civil War. There is a small U.S. Army of about 16,000 professional soldiers ("Regulars") at the beginning of the conflict, but it was not large enough to fight the Confederacy, so large numbers of volunteers are drafted or enlist.

Most Union armies are named after rivers or bodies of water near which they operate—such as the Army of the Potomac or the Army of the Gulf. Below, in alphabetical order, are some of the most prominent Union armies fielded during the war, and the general area of its operations:

- **Army of the Cumberland** (Tennessee and Georgia);
- **Army of the Gulf** (the Gulf of Mexico region);
- **Army of the James** (southeastern Virginia);
- **Army of the Ohio** (Kentucky, Tennessee, and Georgia);
- **Army of the Potomac** (the main Union army in the Eastern Theater of operations; Virginia, Maryland, and Pennsylvania);
- **Army of the Shenandoah** (Shenandoah Valley, Virginia);
- **Army of the Tennessee** (Kentucky, Tennessee, Mississippi, Georgia, and the Carolinas);

Each army is stationed in a department (Department of the East, for example), a geographic area subdivided into districts (District of East Tennessee).

An army includes several different organizational formations, from corps (the largest) to companies (the smallest):*

- **Corps**: made up of two or more divisions, or about 8,000 or more men;
- **Divisions**: three or more brigades, or about 12,000 men;
- **Brigades**: four or more regiments, or about 4,000 men;
- **Regiments**: 10 companies, or 1,000 men;
- **Companies**: 100 men each.*

- Named for the *corps d'armes* of the French Army, an infantry **corps** is usually composed of two or more divisions and includes all arms except cavalry. A cavalry corps is similarly structured and includes various arms but no infantry. A corps is usually commanded by a major general;

- A **division** is the second largest unit in an army. While a division is supposed to contain 8,000 to 12,000 soldiers, the number varies significantly depending upon troops available. It is usually led by a brigadier or major general, but that also varies depending on which generals are killed or wounded, and who is available to replace them. During periods of heavy fighting, for example, lower ranking officers often command larger organizations;

- Union army **brigades** are usually considered the basic tactical infantry unit of the war and commanded by a brigadier general, supported by his aides and the quartermaster, ordnance, commissary, medical, and inspection officers. Some of the famous fighting brigades include the Iron Brigade, the Irish Brigade, the Excelsior Brigade, and the Vermont Brigade;

- An infantry **regiment** is considered a soldier's home away from home because regiments are usually composed of men from the same town or area, which put many related men and prewar friends together in the same outfit. Because the size of companies varies widely, by mid-war a Union infantry regiment numbers only about 350-400. Heavy artillery regiments trained as infantry, but have 12 companies instead of 10, as do cavalry regiments. The regiment is commanded by a colonel, and its officers include a lieutenant colonel, major, adjutant, quartermaster, surgeons, and various non-commissioned officers, such as a sergeant major commissary sergeant.

* The numbers vary widely. Companies are officially organized with 100 men, but because of illness, death, furloughs, and other reasons, they rarely field that number. This is true for every organization.

This Union wagon park was photographed at Brandy Station, Virginia, in May 1864 as the Army of the Potomac was preparing to cross the Rapidan River and confront Robert E. Lee's Army of Northern Virginia in the tangles of the Wilderness. *Author's Collection*

- Each **company** is designated with a letter (Company A, Company B, and so on) from A to K, with the letter "J" omitted (likely because it looks so much like an "I" when written that it might cause confusion). A company is commanded by a captain.

There are other important organizations, without which armies can not function. The Quartermaster Department takes care of field equipment, shelter, and transport, while the Commissary handles food and animal fodder, and the Ordnance Department weapons, such as cannon, muskets, and ammunition.

Campaigning armies are almost always followed by long and cumbersome wagon trains laden with supplies and camp equipment. Rivers are a major means of transporting men and materials to supply depots, where they are moved by boat, train, or wagon to armies operating in the field.

Going to War

The 1861 call for volunteers to put down the rebellion stirs war fever. The coming war is expected to be a short one and young men immediately make plans to go. The first volunteer companies are raised in towns and counties during war meetings complete with fervent speeches and fife and drum music. Young men are urged to do their duty by signing a volunteer muster form. "If you don't sign the roll, John, I will never kiss you again," says one patriotic young miss in admonishing her beau to step forward.

When 100 eligible men volunteer, leaders of the effort offer "a company of volunteers" to the governor. The governor issues commissions and calls for the election of officers. The new companies are ordered to muster camps to be organized into regiments of 10 companies each. These regiments are federalized for service and sent off to active duty.

Left behind are wives, mothers, fathers, siblings, and other family members. The Civil War is a time of absent fathers and brothers, and hard times for many children. It is also a time of great excitement. Young boys dream of being drummers, and others accompany officer fathers to the war front. Those left behind drill with wooden swords and muskets in homemade uniforms. Girls cheer from sidewalks and wave handkerchiefs and join mothers, sisters, and grandmothers to create packages of goods for faraway brothers, fathers, and cousins. Some want to become army nurses. Children's books and magazines of the day are filled with stories and imagery of war.

The Northern volunteers quickly assemble into companies and are sent to be trained. The city boys, shopkeepers, mechanics, farm boys, and hardy lumbermen are a mixed group. A few of the "greenhorn patriots" arrive at the mustering sites dressed in broadcloth and silk hats, while others arrive in red shirts, calico coats, and straw hats. The young volunteers first learn about soldiering in hastily organized state training camps. Each state establishes mustering sites "in close proximity to wood, water and subsistence."

This woodcut depicts a typical war meeting, intended to stir the passions of the listeners and get them to enlist. *Hardtack and Coffee*

The organizing, feeding, equipping, and training of volunteers is a state responsibility until the men go to the front, where they come under Federal authority. Northern states are not prepared to deal with the tens of thousands of early-war volunteers and are forced to scramble to procure uniforms, set up mess halls, and build shelters of canvas and wood. When the new recruits arrive, they find few uniforms, fewer muskets, and very little shelter.

The entire process of becoming a soldier is a rude awakening for these young new volunteers. Their new routine consists of a very structured day designed to make them soldiers:

Daily Routine at Camp Morton at Indianapolis, Indiana	
Reveille: 5:00 a.m.	Signal for dinner: 12:00 p.m.
Roll Call: Immediately after reveille	Battalion drill: 2:30 p.m.
Signal for breakfast: 5:30 a.m.	Dress parade: 5:00 p.m.
Surgeon's call: 6:30 a.m.	Supper call: 6:30 p.m.
Reports and issues: 7:10 a.m.	Retreat: Sunset
Officers' call: 7:40 a.m.	Tattoo: 8:30 p.m.
Guard mounting: 8:00 a.m.	Taps: 10:00 p.m.
Company drill: 9:00 a.m.	

This young girl (right) holds a small photo of her absent soldier-father. Who she was, or whether he ever returned to her, remains unknown. Another father told his wife she should "kiss the babies for me." It was his last letter home before being killed at Antietam. Three Northern women (below) pose before an American Flag in what was considered a patriotic pose that would have inspired their men at the front. *LOC*

It is a time when families separate as husbands, fathers, brothers and sons go to war. One man remembers the departure of his father: "Mother was brave through her tears, and I can imagine my father's going was with a lighter heart because of her bravery and unfaltering courage. The parting was final. They were destined never to meet again."

The movement to the training camps and war front is an adventure as well as frightening for the young volunteers. In faraway rural central Wisconsin, a

New recruits learning the manual of arms. *LOC*

Union soldiers photographed in their militia uniforms in Washington, D.C., in 1861. *LOC*

An early-war Union regiment learning how to march in one of the camps around Washington, D.C. LOC

group of volunteers construct rafts to carry them by river to the nearest railroad to get them to the state's staging area at Camp Randall in Madison. Upon reaching the rail line, they sell the wood of the rafts for spending money that is shared by the raft builders.

For another new soldier the trip to the war front at Washington is his first ride on a train. The speed, noise and smoke add to the excitement, but there is also an anxious moment when the cars pass through his home town. "I have one short view of the place where I have lived for the last 20 years & and then has passed from my sight," one writes in his journal. "I may never again behold the old place, the home of my childhood . . . & if I do it will be one of the happiest moments of my life." He also notes there are citizens standing in groups watching as the train passes, but he did not catch a glimpse of his mother among them.

Camp Life

Soldier life is filled with the monotonous—the same boring routine over and over every day. The men drill long hours on end, construct quarters, dig entrenchments, and stand guard duty. The American armies of 1861 are of a size never seen before on this continent, and feeding, clothing, housing, and providing sanitation and medical attention for so many is a massive undertaking.

During it all, the young soldiers are in camps large and small with comrades and officers from the same hometowns—the familiar and the strange all jumbled together—waiting for something to happen. Letters home—usually very candid and surprisingly literate—often mention food, weather conditions, and the various goings-on in camp. The new volunteers quickly learn that the life of a soldier life is not nearly as exciting as they had expected. Most of their time is spent in camp where every day is filled with drill and then more drill. Each day offers more of the same, a boring effort to just provide themselves with food, shelter, and sanitation. "A military life in camp is the most monotonous in the world," grumbles one new Northern volunteer. "It is the same routine over and over every day."

And, there is the waiting. Soldiers wait for winter to end, for the mail to arrive, for more recruits, for officers to tell them what to do, and for something to happen. To help pass the time, they write letters or read again the letters they received at the last mail call. Since almost all of them are educated to a third grade level, the men turn to newspapers, books, pamphlets, and Bibles to help the hours pass more quickly. They attend church services and play chess, checkers, whist (a card game), and other games, including a popular new one called baseball. Others gamble at dice and cards or seek pastimes they would not write home about.

A group of officers gather to pass the time. Three of the men are smoking cigars, and a box of dominoes is on the rough table before them. *LOC*

Regardless of what they do to pass the time, every new soldier, whether officer or private, wonders about "seeing the elephant"—the euphemism for actual combat. "How will I do in battle?" is a common concern, as is, "Will I make it through alive?"

Camp life brings together thousands of young men who rarely or never traveled far from their home places. Farmers and clerks, banker's sons and immigrant laborers, share the same tents and drill fields. In many ways, those gatherings and armies create a new sense of nation that carries the United States into a new era.

It is also the new game of baseball that has one of the longest reaches on the future. Union soldiers from New York City and surrounding areas introduce it to their new comrades. Thousands of soldiers learn the game and carry it back to faraway hometowns, introducing a wide variety of rules until it eventually becomes "The Nation's Pastime."

These Union men are preparing food for their comrades in camp. *LOC*

Various mascots also help pass the time. They include the usual dogs and roosters as well as the more unusual bear cubs, mules, ponies, and even a pet grey squirrel named "Bunnie." The squirrel is taken in by a squad of soldiers and allowed to run free along the small trees when the men rest. But a fatal accident occurs when the pet jumps from a nearby limb into a camp fire. One soldier calls it a clear case of cremation: "Bunnie did not know what a fire was."

However, it is the pet of the 8th Wisconsin that attracts the most attention—a live bald eagle carried on a perch on a painted shield. The mascot becomes "Old Abe," the famous war eagle, and survives camp life, skirmish and battle, including the fighting at Vicksburg, Mississippi.

Old Abe, the war eagle mascot of the 8th Wisconsin Infantry. Chief Sky of the Chippewa Indians captured Old Abe as a baby eaglet in Wisconsin in 1861. He was later sold to Union volunteers for $2.50.

The eagle was involved in many iconic battles including several fights at Vicksburg. The Confederates despised the mascot bird and officers ordered their men to try and kill it, to no avail. Generals Grant, Sherman, and others were known to tip their hat when passing by the 8th Wisconsin and their loyal mascot.

Old Abe became a national celebrity after the war, but died from smoke inhalation in a fire in 1881. His image became so iconic that it was adopted as the "screaming eagle" on the insignia of the U.S. Army's 101st Airborne Division. *LOC*

African-American teamsters hard at work spend a few minutes to pose for a picture at Bermuda Hundred in Virginia. A signal tower is visible in the background. *LOC*

Enjoying off-duty time, members of the 13th New York Artillery play the new game of baseball near their camp at Petersburg, Virginia. *LOC*

A black cook watches over a campfire late in the war outside Petersburg, Virginia. *LOC*

Hardtack, Pork, and Coffee

Feeding soldiers is complicated by large armies and distant locations. In established camps, fresh cuts of meat, vegetables, and soft bread are issued. Soldiers on the march, however, need more durable food. They live on what they can carry in their haversack—coffee, sugar, salt, hard bread, and salted beef or pork.

Coffee, always popular with the troops, is issued as beans. The beans are pounded or crushed and then boiled with water in tin cups. Hardtack—a square biscuit made of salt, flour, and water—is baked hard. It is often soaked in water and fried in the sizzling fat of the salt pork ration. Says one soldier, "Hard tack

A company cook house. Note the pans, firewood, barrels, and logged (corduroyed) path to negotiate the muddy ground. *LOC*

plain, hard tack fried, hard tack cooked, hard tack crumbled and stewed, or hard tack otherwise compounded."

Regulations call for a daily issue of 16 ounces of hardtack and either 20 ounces of salt beef or 12 ounces of salt pork. The meat is packed in a salty brine solution sufficient to preserve it for two years. By late 1863, desiccated potatoes and vegetables—scalded, then pressed and dried into sheets—are issued to prevent outbreaks of scurvy. The soldiers call them "desecrated vegetables" and generally do not eat them.

The soldier's mess is a part of military life. Rations are generally issued to enlisted men who then cook them individually, or gather to cook and eat in small groups or "messes." In more established camps, the food is prepared by a company cook. However, that arrangement is not always satisfactory. Said one soldier of his cook's qualifications, "Not being able to learn to drill, and too dirty to appear on inspection, he is sent to the cook house to get him out of ranks. We were not sorry when the cook house was abolished."

The Commissary Department and food supply depends on a network of shippers and suppliers to feed the soldiers. It is a network that often stretches far back from the war front.

Wheat from Wisconsin is ground by millers into flour, shipped to the front, and baked into fresh bread in huge army kitchens. Local bakers in Chicago and elsewhere, hundreds of miles away, turn out hardtack packed and shipped in wooden crates. Slaughterhouses in the Upper Middle West butcher thousands of hogs and beef cattle, salt the meat to preserve it, and shipping companies send it into the war zones by the barrel. Livestock dealers move herds of cattle by hoof to provide fresh meat for the soldiers.

All told, this is a very complex logistical system. For example, and generally speaking, it takes eight large beef cattle to supply a full-strength Union brigade of soldiers with fresh meat for one day; 24 for a division, and upwards of 72 to feed a corps.

The wonder at all is that it mostly works, and works fairly well, for as long as it does.

The Winter Months

Winter brings about a pause in active campaigning as the armies are unable to move as freely in the harsh weather, and it is much harder to supply the men and horses.

The winters are trying for all soldiers—and intensely monotonous. The soldiers generally create permanent camps where they construct shelters to wait out the cold months. The necessary acts of supplying food, gathering firewood, and just keeping warm—in addition to the usual inspections and roll calls—take up most of the time.

The layout of infantry, cavalry, and artillery camps is prescribed in regulations. With the approach of winter, the soldiers build log huts with fireplaces, chimneys, and floor boards. The hard wooden bunks are covered with cedar boughs the soldiers jokingly call "Virginia feathers." It "makes the bed a great deal better," one soldier writes home. Regimental camps are often decorated with bough arbors and signs for each company street. The log huts, however, are often ill-suited for their task. "Last night was very stormy," recalls a New York officer. "This morning no better. Our house leaks all over, and our chimney works badly, which make things rather uncomfortable."

The long winter months and inactivity strain morale. Religious revivals are common and help keep morale high. To pass the time, soldiers hold chess and checker tournaments, form singing groups and debating clubs, write letters home, articles for newspapers, and constantly battle the "graybacks" (lice) in their clothing and blankets. Snowball fights offer some excitement, fresh air, and exercise, but mostly life is restricted to the small winter huts. Disease, which kill many more men than lead and iron, is always rampant.

One private remembers of those days, "In November [1861] we crossed the river into Virginia and camped on Arlington Heights… I will never forget that awful winter. The Potomac froze and during the January thaw we were

(Above) A rarely seen view of the men building their winter "shebangs" for winter quarters in 1864 along the James River in Virginia. On the right are some of the unfinished winter huts or cabins. In front of them are recently cut logs. It is hard work, but the men are used to difficult circumstances and life in the field. *LOC*

(Below) A early-war Union camp in Centreville, Virginia, during the winter of 1861-62. Note the wagons bringing in supplies, and the corduroy walkways. *LOC*

A fine example of a late-war winter hut, complete with a shingle roof and windows. *LOC*

compelled to split puncheons and plank our street in order to be able to go from one end to the other, while the blood-thirsty editors at home were asking 'why don't the army move?'" "Mud, mud, mud, precludes everything," an officer writes home.

Soldiers pose before their winter quarters and rows of tents at City Point, Virginia, inside the last line of fortifications. City Point is a major port and staging area late in the war absolutely necessary for supplying the Union armies besieging Richmond and Petersburg. *LOC*

Sick Call and the Quickstep

American medical practices in the Civil War are little improved since the Revolutionary War of 75 years earlier and primitive when compared to advances taking place in Europe. Army doctors are inexperienced and poorly trained, and a medical degree from one of the few medical schools in the United States is not needed to practice medicine.

A surgeon and hospital attendants pose in 1864 near Petersburg, Virginia. Doctors have limited knowledge and little professional training when the war begins, but by 1864 are veterans in caring for the wounded and sick. Sometimes called "butchers" by the soldiers, they do their best for their patients under less than ideal conditions. It is estimated that more than 10,000 doctors serve in the Union Army from 1861-1865. *LOC*

Attendants carry "wounded" soldiers to a military ambulance in this early war staged photograph. Regimental band members are expected to help carry injured men from the battlefield to the four-wheeled ambulances. The ambulances often include a water keg, food, and medicine. LOC

Doctors know little about the effects of drugs and almost nothing about germs. Nearly two-thirds of the deaths in the Civil War are due to disease and infection, not lead and iron. However, anesthesia is widely used during the war, and doctors generally have good surgical instruments with which to operate.

The young volunteer soldiers are especially hard hit by communicable diseases when they arrive at the mustering stations. Men from cities are more like to have been exposed to various germs and so have some level of immunity. It is the boys from rural areas who suffer the most. Whiskey, rest, proper care, and time are the treatments. Malaria—called "the ague" or "the shakes"—accounts for about 20 percent of all sickness during the war. Pneumonia is also common in northern areas. Doctors mostly do not know that pneumonia is caused by germs, and some still believe a patient needs to be bled or that external heat will draw out the illness.

Yellow fever is spread by mosquitoes in swamps, especially along the Mississippi River and near Southern ports. Dysentery, a form of chronic diarrhea, is responsible for one-quarter of all illnesses reported by surgeons. Called "the bloody flux," "the runs," or "the quickstep" by the soldiers, if

Wounded soldiers rest in the shade of a tree following basic treatment at a field hospital near Fredericksburg, Virginia. These soldiers were wounded in the fighting in the Wilderness in early May 1864. Some of the wounded looking at the photographer display bandages. *LOC*

dysentery quickly runs its course the patient usually survives. When the disease lingers, however, death is a more frequent result.

Typhoid is caused by contaminated food and water, and results in fever, diarrhea, and headache. Because these symptoms are similar to dysentery, the treatments are much the same—a variety of mostly ineffective drugs.

Not all wounds are visible. Doctors in the 1860s do not understand or recognize what now is known as Post Traumatic Stress Disorder, or PTSD, but many Civil War soldiers who experience combat will suffer from various symptoms of their traumatic experiences in battle, including nightmares, flashbacks, depression, and a lack of interest in social engagement. They will demonstrate hostile, impulsive behavior, and loud noises trigger reminders of their time in combat. Other veterans will struggle to sleep or concentrate, and experience unease, terror, and aggravation.

After the Civil War, newspapers often carry stories of wandering old soldiers traveling from town to town, sleeping for the night on town squares in their old tents. Others are restless at home, or travel west to seek new lives. The symptoms are often called "soldier's heart" (later called "shell shock" and "battle fatigue"). There is no recognized treatment in the 1860s.

This barn at Keedysville, Maryland, is being used as a hospital after the September 17, 1862, battle of Antietam. All types of structures, including barns, are used as hospitals to house sick and wounded soldiers. One soldier writes that every house, barn, shed, straw stack, rail fence—indeed, anywhere there is shade—has been turned into a medical facility. The tents in the background are probably used by doctors and attendants treating the injured and sick, indicating this location has been used as a hospital for some time. *LOC*

The heat and humidity of the South often proves as deadly as rebel bullets. "I am quite well & in good spirits, but the health of the regiment still continues very poor," writes Sgt. Henry Sholtz of the 38th Iowa from his post in New Orleans. He continued:

> We have but a few men fit for duty. As I wrote to you before of the death of our noble Capt I will say nothing more about it. Both of our lieutenants are sick & the orderly is not well. There are not over fifty men really fit to march now. We lose some every day in the regiment, all from disease contracted at Vicksburg.

Often a soldier will seek a home remedy. One volunteer suffering from diarrhea writes home that he went into the woods in search of bark and roots. "They cured me in two days," he tells his home folk. "So now I am well and feel tip top."

The Wounded and the Dead

Surgeons amputate more arms and legs during the Civil War than any other war involving the United States. Medical advances are slow in coming. Army doctors know surprisingly little about medicine.

The large caliber lead ammunition used during the war causes massive damage to the human body. Because the lead is soft and the bullets fly relatively slowly, the soft lead expands when it hits much of anything, and especially bone. As a result, minie balls break bones into multiple pieces and often splinter them

Hospital treatment of wounded and sick soldiers improve over the course of the Civil War. This posed photograph of the interior of such a facility shows patients enjoying comfortable and clean conditions as they recover. On the far wall, patriotic images lift morale, and beneath them, a soldier sits in an early example of a wheelchair. This hospital, however, is rare, for most during 1861-65 are dark and troubling places. *LOC*

Hospital nurses and surgeons pose for an outdoor image of what is probably a late-war photograph. It is first believed only men should be nurses, but that quickly changes as the war progresses and thousands of men need assistance. At first, females employed as nurses are required to be "plain looking" and "middle-aged." In the final tally, several thousand women will serve as nurses during the war. *LOC*

so badly that doctors have little choice but to amputate the shattered limb. If the limb is not removed, dangerous infection often sets in, including gangrene that then spreads into the blood and brings about a horrible death. At Gettysburg, some surgeons do nothing but cut off arms and legs from dawn until twilight for a week after the fighting.

One of the large scale problems is how to get wounded men off the field and into the hospitals as fast as possible. In the aftermath and confusion of First Bull Run in 1861, a series of reforms are undertaken to hasten and organize the removal of casualties from the battlefield. Dr. Jonathan Letterman organizes an ambulance service, in 1862, for the Army of the Potomac staffed by specially trained soldiers. Under the plan, much like today, stretcher-bearers carry the wounded to primary care stations. They are then loaded into horse-drawn ambulances and transported to field hospitals.

In the Eastern Theater, a network of railroads connect most major cities and help move sick and wounded, but in the Western Theater, rivers are the main transportation arteries. This leads to the development of river steamers

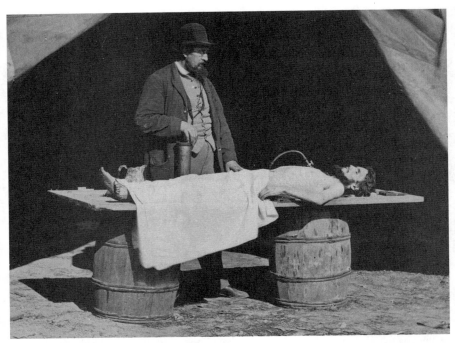

This rather grim posed photo shows an embalming surgeon standing over a dead Union soldier being prepared for a long journey home. The identity of the doctor and the man being embalmed remain unknown. *LOC*

converted to accommodate wounded or sick soldiers and staffed with doctors and nurses.

The more elaborate hospital ships have large water towers that provide hot and cold water for bathing, special drinking faucets on the deck, and even protection from fire. Decks are converted into hospital wards and operating rooms. A large kitchen provides meals delivered by dumbwaiter to different decks, and a steam-operated fan provides air ventilation.

Soldiers who die in battle or from disease are usually carefully buried by friends and comrades from their own companies and regiments. On the battlefield, the dead are buried in their blankets and their graves marked with wooden headboards recording their names and regiments so grieving relatives can finds their body. Coffins are to furnished hospitals and supply areas. Embalmers advertise air-tight, indestructible metallic caskets in which to send loved ones home. Many try to solicit business and pass out flyers to soldiers marching into battle. One firm charges $50 to embalm an officer and $25 for an enlisted man.

Burying the Union dead within the Confederate lines while under a flag of truce at Fredericksburg, Virginia, after the battle there on December 13, 1862. *LOC*

Several thousand women serve as nurses during the war, almost all of them anonymous. Little is known about any of them. Their offers are at first rejected by the military authorities, who believe only men should be nurses. As the war expands, women in large numbers—including nuns—begin providing aid to sick and wounded soldiers in field hospitals, aboard evacuation transports, and in cities and towns across the country. Many work for the Army or the Sanitary Commission while other Northern women travel long distances to volunteer personal care for their sons, husbands and relatives.

Female care-givers wash and feed their charges, read to them, and write their letters. They crusade for competent hospital staff, clean bedding, good food, and better sanitation. At times they are overwhelmed by supply packages from aid societies and well-wishers, and at other times are reduced to foraging for food, medical supplies, and clothing for their suffering patients.

Dorothea Dix and Clara Barton are among the first to organize a nursing corps. One standard Dix adopts for her nurses is that they be "plain looking" and middle-aged. "In those days it was considered indecorous for angels of mercy to appear otherwise than gray-haired and spectacled," explains one young woman who was rejected for the difficult job. "Such a thing as a hospital

A burial part on the battle of Cold Harbor, Virginia, months after the battle. LOC

corps of comely young maiden nurses, possessing grace and good looks, was then unknown." Restrictions on age and looks were quickly overlooked as the war expanded faster than many thought possible, and tens of thousands of men across the country needed care.

In major battles, regimental surgeons set up temporary field stations in nearby barns and buildings. One of the first men to arrive at such a place on July 1, 1863, at Gettysburg is "Mickey" Sullivan of Company K, 6th Wisconsin, Iron Brigade, who has been shot in his shoulder. He recalls the citizens have "wine and refreshments of all kinds on tables and trays, and in their hands, urging them on every wounded man, and assisted them in every way."

Mickey of Company K is dropped off at the courthouse, where he finds Dr. John C. Hall and Dr. O. F. Bartlett of his regiment, along with a large number of civilians "busy cutting up and patching up the biggest part of the sixth regiment." Sullivan is put together "with sticking plaster and bandages" and given coffee. He is among the more fortunate ones there.

Still, he feels faint and lays on the floor and rests. After a time, feeling better, he takes a look around and recalls, "I found nearly every man in my company was in the same fix I was, and some a great deal worse." He finds there his uncle, Hugh Talty, among the injured. Talty—called "Tall T"—is not feeling his wound, for a citizen has filled his canteen with whiskey.

Church and Faith

Religion plays a major role in Civil War armies. As it is today, religion is a largely personal matter. Many soldiers carry their own Bibles and religious objects. The more formal service is left to regimental chaplains, who are usually appointed by the unit commander on the vote of field officers and company commanders. Such chaplains must defer to regularly ordained ministers of a Christian denomination. They receive the pay and allowances of a captain of cavalry.

A religious service in a tent in the 9th Massachusetts Infantry camp near Washington, D.C. in 1861. Religion played an important role in the lives of the soldiers, and chaplains were often assigned to each regiment. This early-war photograph shows soldiers and officers wearing their hats and caps. It was a military tradition to retain headgear while under arms—even for religious services. *LOC*

The chaplains oversee the moral condition of the men in their regiments, conduct Sunday services, and assist at the burial of soldiers. Conscientious chaplains also visit hospitals and guard houses and minister to the individual needs of soldiers. Military officials make regular efforts to weed out the incompetent, but are often unsuccessful. The proportion of Catholic to Protestant chaplains is one to 20, although Catholic historians believe the ratio of their faith to Protestants in the Army was at least one in six. There is little friction between the Catholic and Protestant chaplains, and most men of the cloth are regarded as sincere, hard-working religious men.

Army chaplains are generally a great comfort, especially for homesick soldiers or those about to go into battle. One of the Iron Brigade chaplains tending Battery B of the 4th U.S. Artillery is remembered as a pious man who is "always at hand when the boys were double shooting, sleeves rolled up, working their guns to the best."

As he watches, one gunner steps back before firing, telling comrades, "Now boys, give 'em hell!"

The clergyman quickly reprimands the gunner. "How do you expect to have the support of Divine Providence when you use such language?"

The gunner gives the chaplain a hard look. "To hell with the Divine Providence, the Iron Brigade supports us," he says. Or at least, that is how the story is told long after the war.

Another soldier writes of his chaplain leaving the army to go home: "Being as he was not liked he will not be missed. He has never done the Regiment the first particle of good. He preached but a very few sermons and then did not amount to but very little. What little he did was for the benefit of his pocket, not for the Regiment."

Discipline and Good Order

Good discipline is critical to a regiment's performance, and the overall health of an army, and increases morale. Lack of discipline ranges from drunkenness and rowdy behavior to outright mutiny. Absenteeism is a major problem throughout the war. Homesickness drives many soldiers to desert, though most eventually return to their regiments. Those that do not return face an increasing risk of execution as the war went on.

Many disciplinary problems stem from the volunteers' belief that the best soldier is one "whose good sense tells him when to be merely a part of a machine and when not." Regular army officers take a dim view of this notion, and common infractions are often met with physical punishments, some severe. Extra guard duty, confinement, use of the ball and chain, forfeiture of pay, and

Union troops are gathered outside Petersburg, Virginia, to witness the execution of one of their own. LOC

reduction in rank are common, though one new recruit is fined $10 for calling his sergeant "a bad name."

Death by firing squad or hanging is used to punish serious offenses such as desertion, treason, or heinous crimes like murder. Regimental commanders also use a wide range of lesser punishments to deal with minor disciplinary problems. Most of the common punishments on the regimental level involve loss of pay or time in a guardhouse.

Other disciplinary actions include:

Riding the Wooden Horse (right): The body of the "horse" is narrow and high so the misbehaving soldier's feet could not touch the ground.

The Ball and Chain: An iron ball is attached by a heavy chain to the soldier's ankle.

Strapped to a Stick: The "stick" is a large log tied behind the head and across the shoulders.

Bucked and Gagged (left): A bayonet or stick is placed in the soldier's mouth with a string behind the head holding it in place. The man is seated on the ground with his knees drawn up, a piece of wood under his knees. His arms are placed under the wood on each side of the knees and his hands are tied in front.

Riding the Wheel (right): Some soldiers were tied to a spare wheel, their legs drawn apart until they spanned three spokes and their arms stretched about the same distance. Moderate punishment might be several hours like this; severe punishment included the turning of the wheel, which could cause excruciating pain.

Hanging by the Thumbs: An uncomfortable punishment that ties the hands above the soldier and forces him to stand on his toes, often for hours at a time. *Harper's Weekly*

Even the threat of severe discipline does not always deter misbehavior. One of the many expedients adopted by regimental sutlers is selling contraband liquor to soldiers. "They drop a couple of peaches into a bottle of whisky, and sell the compound as 'pickled peaches.' A more irreverent expedient is to have a tin made and painted like a hymn book and labeled *The Bosom Companion*."

In the final tally, it takes a long while to learn that discipline, morale, and ability of a regiment (and even an army), depends on the ability of its officers to keep their men in control and out of trouble.

The War and Technology

Technology steps ahead of the tactics and experience at the start of the Civil War and the officers of both sides are slow to catch up. Some of the "firsts" of the war include the use of railroads to move troops, land mines, ironclad vessels such as the USS *Monitor* and CSS *Virginia*, hot-air balloons for

One of the military balloons used by Professor Thaddeus Lowe for aerial observation outside Richmond near Gaines Mill, Virginia, in the spring of 1862. Lowe initially used the balloons shortly after First Bull Run to gather information on Confederate positions south of the Potomac River. His most famous balloon was the *Intrepid*. Lowe's balloons made some 3,000 assents, but when his role was reduced he resigned his position in May 1863 and left military service. *LOC*

(Above) After a Civil War battle, the ground was strewn with debris including thousands of dropped or fired lead bullets and portions of burst artillery shells. This photo shows a piece of shell from a rifled artillery piece and several bullets recovered from the Gettysburg battlefield in Pennsylvania. *Author*

(Below) The fragile paper cartridges with powder and ball are carried in a leather cartridge box suspended from a shoulder sling. To keep them dry, a tin insert was placed inside the boxes. The leather pouches were designed to carry 40 cartridges—20 loose on the top of the tin and two packets of 10 each in the lower area of the tins. *Author*

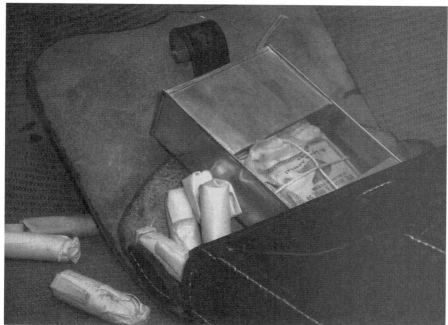

A Union cavalry detail is assigned to guard these boxcars at a busy railroad depot at Chattanooga, Tennessee. The guards show the importance given to the movement of supplies by rail during the Civil War. A locomotive with its distinctive smoke stack is in the foreground. *LOC*

aerial observation, and even a machine gun called the Gatling gun. There are also major improvements in medicine and nursing, the imposition of an income tax, and an unpopular draft to provide men for the armies.

One of the foremost innovations is the new "rifle-musket," which becomes the standard issue for both armies. Rifles have long been used in war but slow to load, so the basic infantry firearm until the mid-19th century is the muzzle-loading, smoothbore musket. The smoothbore is quick to load, but its effective range is limited. The new .58-caliber rifle-musket (with the length of a musket and the rifling of the rifle) is adopted for U.S. service in 1855, just six years before the start of the Civil War. It is still a muzzle-loader, but has grooves in the barrel to spin and stabilize a new hollow-based bullet called the

"Minie-ball," and produces surprising accuracy and velocity to several hundred yards and more.

Two breech-loading repeating shoulder arms—the Spencer and Henry— change the face of war. Both use ready-made bullets inserted into a loading tube. Chambering of a round is done by working a lever for the Henry or the trigger guard for the Spencer. First patented in 1860, the Spencer is capable of 15 shots per minute compared with just three shots for the single-shot, muzzle-loading rifled musket. The 15-shot Henry is the forerunner of the modern lever-action carbines of today. Unfortunately, Union military ordnance officers prevent wide adoption of the repeaters, arguing the men would simply waste ammunition and the cost would be too great. By the end of the Civil War, the muzzle-loading shoulder arm is obsolete.

Nothing shouts Civil War "technology" louder than the development of ironclad warships. This photo shows the deck and turret of the ironclad USS *Monitor* on the James River in Virginia in 1862. The *Monitor* was one of the most important vessels in all of naval history. The turret shows some of the damage suffered during its famous battle against the Confederate ironclad *Virginia* at Hampton Roads, Virginia, March 9, 1862. After the four-hour fight, the *Virginia* returned to its base at Norfolk. Both ships suffered cruel fates. The Rebels destroyed the *Virginia* when the important port of Norfolk was captured. The *Monitor* sunk off North Carolina on December 31, 1862. It was discovered and the turret and other relics have been raised and preserved. *LOC*

Load in Nine Counts

The typical Civil War rifle-musket of the Springfield Armory model is 58 ½ inches long with a 40-inch rifled barrel. It weighs 9 ¼ pounds when equipped with an 18-inch socket bayonet. It is capable of putting 10 consecutive shots in a four-inch bull's-eye at 100 yards and 10 consecutive shots in a 27-inch bull's-eye at 500 yards. At 1,000 yards, the bullet still has the power to penetrate four inches of soft pine wood. It is muzzle-loaded, and Northern troops are usually taught to use a very complicated nine-count procedure to load it. A trained infantryman can fire two or three aimed shots per minute:

1. Load

2. Handle Cartridge! (Seize the cartridge with the thumb and next two fingers, and place it between the teeth.)

3. Tear Cartridge! (Tear the paper to the powder.)

4. Charge Cartridge! (Empty the powder into the barrel.)

5. Draw Rammer! (Draw rammer, place head on the ball.)

6. Ram Cartridge! (Press the ball home.)

7. Return Rammer! (Return rammer under the barrel.)

8. Prime! (Raise musket and place a cap from the pouch on the firing cone.)

9. Shoulder Arms! (Await the command to aim and fire.)

It is very important for soldiers to learn how to load and fire weapons in an organized, methodical, and calm fashion, especially under the stress and strain of battle. Firm discipline in this regard often make the difference between holding a position or losing it.

Despite all the drills regarding the loading and firing of rifled muskets, it was discovered after battles that many men did not fire their weapons in battle at all. Small arms picked up off battlefields and examined are found to have multiple bullets rammed down the barrel, one atop the next. In the heat and excitement of battle, many soldiers think they are firing their weapons, when in fact they are not! But they keep loading! Some may have forgotten to put a priming cap on the firing cone or simply failed to pull the trigger. Ramrods are also left in the barrels and fired at the enemy by mistake.

War is a stressful business, indeed.

Cavalry to the Front!

A young volunteer faced with a choice of service often considers the cavalry over the infantry and artillery because of its aura of storied dash and bravery. Recruits in the mounted units quickly discover, however, the reality of cavalry life is far different from their romantic ideals.

Mobility allows mounted units to perform tasks foot soldiers can't do or do as well. This includes reconnaissance and screening efforts, escort duties, carrying messages, defensive and delaying actions, the vigorous pursuit and harassment of defeated enemy commands, offensive feints and attacks, and, of course, long-distance raiding against lines of communications, supply depots, fixed positions, telegraph lines, railroads, wagon trains, and other vulnerable targets. All of these are grueling and exhausting. One horse soldier writes home, "I had a dim notion about the 'romance' of a soldier's life [when I enlisted]. I have bravely got over it since."

Despite the daily routine duties, however, the cavalry still wins its share of fame during the Civil War. This is not true during the war's early years, when Confederate cavalry is much better handled and led than its Union counterparts. One embarrassment follows another until early June 1863, when a revitalized Northern mounted arm surprises Jeb Stuart's Confederate troopers and fights them to a stand-still. Although they are driven back, the Union cavalry make a statement that day at Brandy Station. From that point through the end of the war in 1865, Union cavalry is ascendant. Quality leaders like John Buford, Phil Sheridan, David Gregg, Wesley Merritt, James Wilson, and many others, together with good mounts and quality equipment, carry the day and help the Union win the war.

A well-equipped cavalryman and his mount. (above). One of the popular songs of the era includes the refrain, "If you want to have a good time—jine the cavalry!" This booted horse soldier carries a Model 1860 cavalry saber, while his horse is equipped with what is called a "McClellan Saddle," a design suggested by Union Major General George McClellan based on a style in use in Europe. *LOC*

George Armstrong Custer (right), a brash, young, and aggressive cavalry leader, led troops through most of the war. His luck would run out in 1876 along the Little Bighorn. *LOC*

This confident and well-armed cavalry soldier is ready to face the enemy as he poses for a photograph. In addition to the large saber, he carries a percussion revolver in his belt and a Model 1860 Army Colt (with an attached shoulder stock) in his hand. Unfortunately, his unit and name, as well as his fate as a soldier, are lost to history. *LOC*

At Gettysburg, Union cavalrymen are involved in the opening and ending of the battle. Fighting dismounted northwest of the town, Federal horse soldiers under John Buford wage a brilliant delaying action against the Confederate infantry advance on the morning of July 1, 1863. Arguably, the most storied Union mounted unit is the Michigan Cavalry Brigade, under a young blonde-haired cavalier general named George Armstrong Custer, which plays a prominent role in the fighting on the third and final day on July 3. Jeb Stuart's Confederate cavalry operates beyond the Union right flank and runs into Union horsemen there, fighting a large pitched and bloody mounted action on East Cavalry Field.

During the Vicksburg Campaign of 1863, General Grant authorizes a number of diversions. One is led by Benjamin Grierson, whose cavalry moves south out of Tennessee down through Mississippi on a brilliant raid that sows chaos and captures supplies while taking the focus off Grant's army as it marches south in Louisiana to cross the Mississippi River below Vicksburg and move inland against the city.

A classic example of pursuit by cavalry includes the Union mounted effort under Phil Sheridan during the war's final days during the Appomattox Campaign. The union cavalrymen destroy Southern food supplies, weaken General Lee's exhausted command, and impede his route of march.

All of these examples (and others) demonstrate the evolution of the use of cavalry, which changes radically during the American Civil War.

The Long-Arm: Civil War Artillery

Artillery is in a state of transition at the start of the Civil War. The field pieces and siege guns used in 1861 are generally muzzle-loaded and little-changed from the Napoleonic era. However, rifling (twisting barrel grooves in the tube) is being introduced, and breech-loaders are being developed in Europe.

The artillery ("long-arm") is used against enemy infantry formations, to bombard buildings, break apart fortifications, and to sink ships (either from

(Facing Page) Union soldiers pose with a captured Confederate artillery piece after the fall of Atlanta, Georgia, in September 1864. The gun—a 12-lb. Bronze Napoleon—is designed for open field use, but is in this case formed part of a Rebel defensive line. The earthworks use deep enclosures to provide maximum protection. *LOC*

shore forts or ship to ship). In most cases, artillery fights together with the infantry on the battlefield, although who controls the guns changes as the war progresses.

The most common piece for both sides is the Napoleon, which fires a 12-pound spherical shell with a timed fuse and is effective up to a range of 1,500 yards. The rifled Parrott gun is accurate to 2,500 yards. In addition to solid shot, guns fire bursting shells using a timed fuse, and canister, a thin iron can full of lead or iron balls packed in sawdust. Canister is an anti-personnel weapon used primarily against infantry at close ranges, much like a blast of a giant shotgun.

Each gun and limber is normally drawn by a team of six horses harnessed two abreast. The teams are controlled by three drivers who ride the left horses. Each gun is usually accompanied by caisson carrying two ammunition chests with a spare wheel attached to the rear chest.

Both Union and Confederate forces also deploy mortars, heavy, squat weapons used to lob shells by high-angle fire—ideal for siege operations. In all,

(Above) Large mortars (like these outside Yorktown in Virginia in 1862) are used in siege warfare. They are among the oldest forms of artillery and did not change much over the centuries. They throw a fused shell in a high arc above enemy fortifications. This mortar uses a 13-inch shell weighting 220 lbs. that can be fired as far as 4,325 yards. *LOC*

(Above) The workhorse piece of both sides is the 12-lb. smoothbore artillerymen call a "Napoleon" (after French Emperor Louis Napoleon). The bronze gun is highly maneuverable and very reliable. The Rebels make a similar iron model. (Below) Parrott Rifles (like these of the 1st New York Artillery, Pettit's Battery, outside Richmond) had a reinforcing band of iron at the breech. The style is developed by Robert Parrott, an 1824 graduate of the U.S. Military Academy at West Point, New York. Note the mud on the wheel and carriage. There are many types of Parrotts, which are one of the most widely used rifled pieces of the Civil War. *LOC*

Soldiers attached to the 3rd Massachusetts Heavy Artillery man one of the many forts ringing Washington, DC. Their large Parrott artillery piece is very heavy, and not easily moved. Because of that, it is mounted on a track to allow them to swing it from side to side. *LOC*

more than 50 different types and sizes of cannons are used in the Civil War. The most unusual is the breech-loading Whitworth gun made in England, which is capable of accurately firing a solid shot as far as five miles. Some of the larger guns become so famous they are given names, such as "The Dictator" and "Swamp Angel," two large siege mortars.

The basic Union unit of artillery in the Civil War is a battery of four to six guns with 70 to 100 artillerymen commanded by a captain. Eight cannoneers are needed to fire each field piece. A light battery also needs 110 horses to pull the unit's cannons, limbers, caissons, forge wagon, and supply wagons—as well as food for the horses themselves.

A 10-pound Parrott rifled barrel used in 1861 is 78 inches long and weighs 908 pounds. The total weight of the barrel and carriage is 1,799 pounds. The Parrott fires a 10-pound, 2.9-inch diameter projectile.

The two-wheeled limber carriage hauls an ammunition chest full of shells directly connected behind a team of six horses towing a gun or caisson. The two-wheel caisson carries two more ammunition chests and a spare wheel.

General Henry H. Hunt, a West Point graduate of the U.S. Military Academy and a career artillery officer, is the most famous Federal artillery officer of the Civil War. Other prominent artillery officers in Union service include John Gibbon, Alonzo Cushing (who is killed in at the Angle at

A Short Glossary of Artillery Terms:

Gun: The common name for a cannon, a long-barreled gun which shot large caliber projectiles in a straight flat trajectory;

Mortar: A short-barred gun which shot large caliber projectiles in a high, arching trajectory;

Smoothbore: The inside of the barrel was like a smooth tube. It had a shorter effective range than a rifled gun;

Rifled: The inside of the barrel had grooves cut into it, forcing the ammunition to spin like a football. It was more accurate and had a greater range than a smoothbore;

Muzzle Loader: Loaded down the muzzle, or front, of the barrel;

Breech Loader: Loaded from the rear. Two of the most commonly used pieces were the 12-pound Napoleon, a smoothbore bronze muzzle-loader, and the 10-pound iron Parrott Rifle, one of the first true rifled guns.

Gettysburg at the height of Pickett's Charge), Charles E. Hazlett, and Charles S. Wainwright.

One of the dangers of serving in the artillery is working around caissons and limbers full of extra gunpowder and artillery shells, which are prone to explode when struck by enemy rounds.

Because of the day's technology, artillery is generally limited to firing at targets the gunners could see, something known as "direct" fire. Early in the war, however, Union hot-air balloons are occasionally used to spot Confederate targets. They share the information by using signal flags to the gunners below—an example of "indirect" fire.

The Navy

The Union navy is very small at the beginning of the war and consists of just 42 commissioned vessels. The Lincoln administrations set two long-term goals: blockade and inland superiority.

Blockade: The Confederacy has a long meandering coastline some 2,500 miles long; much of it needs to be patrolled and its major seaports like Charleston, Wilmington, Savannah, and New Orleans, choked off from the outside world. It is a tough assignment, but over time and with the addition of more warships, the blockade slowly strangles the South's economy.

The river-based USS *Louisville* participated in the Fort Donelson campaign in Tennessee, the reduction of Island No. 10 and New Madrid and the battle of Memphis on the Mississippi River, and helped capture Fort Hindman in Arkansas. In April 1863, she ran the Vicksburg batteries and shelled Grand Bluff. After the Red River campaign she was decommissioned. Four crew members were awarded the Medal of Honor. *LOC*

Seamen Ebenezer McKay (1833-1920). *LOC*

In March of 1862 the blockade of the James River in Virginia leads to the battle of Hampton Roads, where the USS *Monitor* battled the CSS *Virginia* to a standstill in the world's first battle of ironclads. Other efforts at closing ports leads to loss of Southern forts like Pulaski in Savannah, Forts Jackson and St. Philip off New Orleans, and later in the war, Fort Fisher in North Carolina.

Brown Water Navy: The second major goal is to build a fleet of river-based gunboats and transports to support inland army campaigns. It is not until 1862 that a fleet of such gunboats (which are usually under Army control and so technically not part of the United States Navy) is ready to support Federal forces moving from Illinois south down the Mississippi River, and along other rivers in Tennessee, and elsewhere into the heart of the South. The vessels are little more than flat-bottomed, steam-driven barges clad in iron or more often, heavy timber (and in some cases, protected by cotton bales and thus called "cottonclads"), but they enable the strategic penetration of the Confederacy via the western rivers.

A young man wishing to join the Union Navy needs parental consent if he is under 18 and no one under the age of 13 is accepted. A volunteer needs to be at least 5-feet-8 inches. No man without naval experience is accepted over the age of 33 unless he has a trade, and then 38 years is the limit.

Before the war, the Navy tries to restrict the number of African Americans in service to 1/20th of the crew. However, the pressure of the blockade duty

Sailors on deck of the ironclad USS *Monitor* on James River in Virginia in early 1862. The turret shows damage from its recent fight with the CSS *Virginia*. The four-hour exchange of fire marks the beginning of the end for wooden warships. Many of these men drown off Cape Hatteras, North Carolina, when the *Monitor* sinks on December 31, 1862. The wreck was found in 1973 and the turret raised and preserved. *LOC*

A "powder monkey" stands next to a Parrott Rifle aboard the USS *New Hampshire* off Charleston, South Carolina. Young sailors carry gunpowder from the powder magazine in the ship's hold to guns. Powder monkeys are usually 12 to 14 years old and selected for their speed and height. It is a very dangerous and important job. *LOC*

results in a high percentage of blacks, including free men and runaways, in the lower ranks. A recent study estimates about 18,000 African-American men and a dozen African-American women serve in the Union navy during the Civil War, or about 15 percent of the total enlisted.

Following a brief stay aboard a training ship, new sailors are placed on duty on a variety of vessels ranging from sea going blockading ships to smaller, low-draft river craft. Pay scales range from $12 a month for inexperienced hands to $18 a month for seamen. Boys are paid from $7 to $9 a month depending on ability and experience.

Despite all the necessary duties required on any ship, boredom is the biggest problem. There is very little ship-to-ship combat over the four years of

Admiral David Farragut, famous for shouting "Damn the torpedoes! Full speed Ahead!" as his fleet of Union gunboats enter heavily fortified Mobile Bay, Alabama, in August 1864. The *Tennessee*, a powerful Confederate ironclad, is captured, and the land forts fall. Mobile was the last major port on the Gulf of Mexico east of the Mississippi River still in Southern hands, so its control terminates blockade-running there and helps secure the reelection of President Lincoln. *LOC*

the war, and for the majority of men time passes slowly. Sailors eagerly look forward to short periods of liberty on shore. Some seamen slip into despondency performing the same duty day after day. One naval surgeon called the condition "land sickness."

Ultimately, the U.S. Navy plays a large role in defeating the Confederacy. The blockade becomes increasingly effective and by the last year of the war is seriously crippling the South. Naval support at City Point, Virginia, provides key logistical support for General Grant's siege of Richmond and Petersburg. Naval actions along inland rivers, and especially in the Gulf of Mexico and along the Mississippi River, help capture New Orleans, Vicksburg, and Port Hudson. In early 1865, navy ships land troops that storm and capture Fort Fisher, the key to the important port of Wilmington, North Carolina.

The North could not have won the war without the U.S. Navy, whose role is often overlooked.

An Emancipation Proclamation

W hy did the Northern men enlist early in the Civil War to fight Southern men from the same country?

Billy Yank joins for a host of reasons. Some to defend the Union by fighting. Others join because it is a chance of a lifetime to do something they think is glorious in faraway lands they otherwise will never see. Immediately after Fort Sumter, relatively few sign their enlistment papers to risk their lives to free slaves. How Billy Yank views African-Americans, thinks of the institution of slavery, and why they fight changes—and sooner than anyone thinks.

The new Union volunteers look into the hard face of slavery during the first months of the war. The columns pushing out of Washington are met by thousands of fugitives bound for freedom. As armies move, in the east and in the west, the crowds of fugitives follow, gathering in makeshift camps near Lincoln's soldiers simply because they do not know where else to go.

Senior officers have no idea what to do about them—there is no official policy for dealing with runaway slaves, and no plan to house and feed them. Indeed, the army has never faced such a situation. Men in the lower ranks do not have this problem. From the very first, the ex-slaves cook and wash for the soldiers, tend horses and mules, drive wagons, erect tents, and a perform a host of other tasks for food, coins, and for freedom.

Despite some harsh treatment here and there, the runaways are soon a fundamental part of army life. A quick look at the old photographs shows evidence of this. In the background of hundreds of the images, stand black cooks, teamsters, and camp helpers in twos or threes, looking into the camera from afar with sober faces. Billy Yank volunteers accept them from the first, and in hard soldier fashion take to calling them "contrabands"—a name made famous by the infamous Union General Benjamin Butler, who describes fugitives reaching his camp as "contraband of war."

A reenactment of Abraham Lincoln signing the Emancipation Proclamation on July 22, 1862, painted by Francis B. Carpenter at the White House in 1864. Left to right: Edwin M. Stanton, Secretary of War, Salmon P. Chase, Secretary of the Treasury, President Lincoln, Gideon Welles, Secretary of the Navy, Caleb B. Smith, Secretary of the Interior, William H. Seward, Secretary of State, Montgomery Blair, Postmaster General, and Edward Bates, Attorney General. Simon Cameron and Andrew Jackson are featured as paintings. *LOC*

Within not too many months, many of the runaways, freed men, and others are also in blue uniforms themselves. Often overlooked is a simple truth: from the months of the Civil War until its end, ex-slaves are as much a part of the fabric of the Union army as the soldiers themselves.

Following the Union victory at Antietam, President Lincoln announces an "Emancipation Proclamation" in late 1862 that changes everything. Slaves in the states still in rebellion on January 1, 1863, it states, "will be then, thenceforward, and forever free." This is a turning point in the Civil War.

The Proclamation accomplishes little that is not already happening. The Federal soldiers are already creating freedom and ending slavery wherever they march. As a political statement, however, the document is far-reaching in its consequences. It not only changes the reason why the Union armies remain in the field, but makes it politically impossible for countries like England and France, who have already abandoned slavery, to support a Confederacy fighting to keep it.

This remarkable photograph shows African-American men, women, and children seated in front of and inside a mule-drawn covered wagon. Artist Alfred Waud worked up a sketch from this photograph on January 1, 1863. The drawing is called "An arrival in Camp—under the Proclamation of Emancipation," and published in *Harper's Weekly*, on January 31, 1863. LOC

Billy Yank gives the document a decidedly mixed reception. Many do not know what to make of it or where it will lead the nation. One soldier calls it "that great paper," and says it will always "be associated with the history of Mr. Lincoln's Administration." Others fear or despise it. Some bitterly proclaim this political document moves beyond the original reason they joined in the first place—and it was not to free slaves. Others lament that the Proclamation will only stiffen Confederate resistance and derail any chance for a negotiated settlement that might restore the Union.

Before too long, Billy Yank generally accepts the Proclamation. It will, one officer explains in a letter home, "make hard times for a while, but it will forever settle the everlasting slavery question." Another soldier tells an Ohio audience, "We are hailed everywhere by the Negroes as their deliverers. They all know that 'Mass Linkum' has set them free, and I never saw one not disposed to take advantage of the fact. . . . We like the Proclamation because it lets the whole world know what the real issue is. . . . We like the Emancipation Proclamation because it is right."

The Proclamation also opens the way for Federal regiments organized with black soldiers, and allows Indians in Western states to be drafted, accept bounty money, and enlist in existing regiments. All such service— despite widespread acceptance of black soldiers during the Revolutionary War—was previously discouraged by claims it is "a white man's war."

The Union armies in 1863 begin formally organizing African-American regiments as U.S. Colored organizations. Even in uniform the new soldiers find injustice. They are paid less ($10 a month instead of $13), and at first cannot fight but are used to garrison distant posts and for menial labor. It is not until 1864 that Congress passes a bill authorizing equal pay for black and white soldiers.

By the end of the Civil War, some 180,000 - 200,000 black men serve— about 10 percent of the Union armies. About 10,000 black soldiers die in battle, and another 30,000 from illness or infection. Many of the U.S. Colored regiments—such as the 54th Massachusetts, depicted in the movie Glory—are cited for bravery and good service.

United States Colored Troops

The recruitment of African-Americans to serve in Union regiments is not looked upon favorably by most Federal officials, at least initially. It takes hold, though, and several outfits of black soldiers is organized as state militia units with white officers.

On May 22, 1863, the Federal government created the Bureau of Colored Troops. These regiments of Colored Troops (United States Colored Troops, or U.S.C.T.) will serve in every theater of the war, primarily as garrison and rearguard troops, before returning home in October 1865. By the time the Civil

A detachment of African American soldiers rests in 1863 near the Aiken House at Aiken's Landing in Virginia. Official U.S. Colored units are not allowed until 1863. More than 200,000 blacks serve in the Union army and navy during the Civil War. LOC

Sgt. Tom Strawn, Co. B, Third United States Colored Heavy Artillery, poses with both a musket and a Remington percussion revolver in front of a painted backdrop showing a mortar and a cannon. Strawn and his comrades serve as garrison troops at Fort Pickering on Winter Island off Massachusetts, and in the sprawling defenses around Memphis, Tennessee, in 1864-65. *LOC*

War ends, black enlisted troops, led by white officers, are a critically important part of the Union war effort.

The U.S.C.T. participates in several major battles. The 54th Massachusetts, led by white officer Robert Gould Shaw, fights in the unsuccessful storming of Battery Wagner in Charleston on July 11, 1863 (as depicted in the movie Glory). The dead are unceremoniously dumped into a shall mass grave, into which the corpse of Shaw is also thrown and buried. Black troops take part in the controversial fighting at Fort Pillow, where Confederate General Nathan Bedford Forrest is alleged to have killed large numbers who try to surrender, and also in the Battle of Nashville, in December 1864, which destroys the Southern Army of Tennessee and ends the invasion of Tennessee.

Perhaps the most famous pitched battle involving black troops is at the Battle of the Crater during the Petersburg Campaign on July 31, 1864, when the Union army digs a long tunnel under no-man's-land to the Confederate works, packs the end with explosives, and sets it off. Although U.S.C.T. units have trained for this effort, they are swapped out at the eleventh hour for other white troops because top generals are afraid that if the black troops are slaughtered, especially in such a risky effort, it will look as though they were being advanced in front to absorb casualties. By the time the U.S.C.T. are thrown in the battle is already as good as lost. Some Confederates, when they realize they are fighting black troops, do not take prisoners or allow men to surrender.

Black troops, mostly former slaves serving with the 41st U.S.C.T., are present at Appomattox Courthouse when General Robert E. Lee's Army of Northern Virginia surrenders on April 9, 1865.

Prisoners of War

The North and South do not have a policy on prisoners of war in 1861 for two basic reasons. First, most men on both sides do not think the war will last long; second, the Union does not want to do anything that might be seen as officially recognizing the existence of the Confederacy. When the South captures more than 1,000 Union soldiers at First Bull Run in July 1861, however, public opinion forces a change and informal exchanges begin.

In 1862, both sides meet and agree to formalize exchanges and paroles in what is called the Dix-Hill Cartel. Men are exchanged as quickly as possible for their equivalent on the other side—a private for a private, a sergeant for a sergeant, and a captain for a captain (though a navy captain or an army colonel is deemed to be worth 15 privates or ordinary seamen). Only then can both prisoners rejoin their units and fight. After 10 days, however, men not exchanged must be paroled on the promise they will not serve in any military capacity unless or until they are exchanged.

The arrangement breaks down in 1863 when Confederate officials refuse to exchange or parole African-American prisoners because most were former slaves and so do not belong to the Union army but to their former masters. The Confederacy threatens to treat them as slaves and execute their white officers for insurrection. By August 1863, large-scale exchanges have largely ceased. The establishment of prison camps, and large numbers of prisoners, begins in earnest. Hundreds of thousands of men will be captured before the war ends. Of those, more than 30,000 Union and 26,000 Confederates will die in captivity.

Almost every prison—whether in the North or the South—leaves behind a sordid record. Andersonville in Georgia is perhaps the worst of the Confederate camps. On November 10, 1865, the Confederate commandant of the Andersonville prison, Henry Wirz, is hanged in the yard of the Old Capital Prison in Washington for war crimes.

(Above) Union prisoners at notorious Camp Sumter, better known as Andersonville, in Southern Georgia. The open stockade was 1,620 feet by 779 feet and opened in February 1864. At its height, nearly 32,000 prisoners were jammed within its walls. Andersonville National Cemetery includes 12,912 graves, 921 of which are "unknown." *LOC*

(Below) The hanging of Henry Wirz, Andersonville prison's commandant, on November 10, 1865, at the Old Capitol Prison in Washington, DC (the present site of the Supreme Court building). His neck did not break, and so he slowly strangled to death. Wirz was the only man hanged for war crimes. *LOC*

Death rates in the many prisons vary. A higher percentage of men die in Southern prisons than in Union camps. Some 12% of the Confederates held in Northern prisons die, compared to 15.5% for those held in Southern prisons. However, the Union prison at Camp Douglas in Chicago, has a death rate of about 20%.

One of the North's most unusual prison camps is established on Johnson's Island in Lake Erie in Sandusky Bay north of Ohio. It includes barracks and outbuildings and is used chiefly for Confederate officers. More than 15,000 Southern prisoners are held there during a three-year period. The island today includes a Confederate cemetery with about 300 graves.

The Union's westernmost prisoner of war camp is at Rock Island, a swampy piece of land in the Mississippi River between Davenport, Iowa, and Rock Island, Illinois. It consists of 84 barracks with limited water and poor drainage. The new camp is not even complete when 5,000 prisoners arrive there in December 1863. Of the 12,409 men confined during the prison's 19 months of operation, 1,960 prisoners and 171 guards die from disease.

Drafted and Bounty Men

As the war drags on and the need for soldiers becomes more acute, President Abraham Lincoln signs a March 3, 1863, act requiring that all men between 18 and 45 be enrolled into local militia units for possible call to Federal service. Several occupations—telegraph operators, judges, and government employees—are exempted; also excluded are men with mental or physical disabilities, such as lack of sight in the right eye and missing fingers. Included in the latter are men with missing front teeth and molars because they are unable to bite open the paper musket cartridges of the day.

The actual "drafting" is done by individual states. Each state is given a quota based on population. Volunteers are deducted from the overall quota and the difference drafted. To avoid the draft and meet their quotas, some local communities offer bounties to enlistees as high as $700. To put this in perspective, the price of an 80-acre frontier farm at the time is about $300. The practice is not always successful because "bounty jumpers" enlist just to collect their bounty and then desert and enlist somewhere else to collect another bounty.

A drafted man can be exempted from the draft by paying $300 or by hiring a substitute to serve in his place. Unscrupulous substitute agents will often gather unwary volunteers by paying lesser amounts to individuals unaware of the $300 payment. Foreigners, especially in the Germanic and Irish communities, oppose the draft and renounce their intent to become citizens. Many catch what is called "Canadian Fever" and flee north while others go west into the territories out of the reach of draft agents.

The draft is wildly unpopular. The first major draft disturbance of the Civil War occurs November 10, 1862, in Port Washington, Wisconsin. State Commissioner William A. Pors encounters an unruly mob chanting, "No draft! No draft!" The crowd includes many immigrants who oppose the war, the draft,

These men are standing in front of a recruitment office for the U.S. Navy with a sign offering a "Bounty" of "$500! Prize Money!" They are looking for men to enlist in the navy for the bonuses offered by local, state, or Federal agencies. *LOC*

and compulsory military service. A full-blown riot breaks out, and the commissioner is pushed down the courthouse stairs, pummeled, kicked, pelted with rocks, and flees for his life.

The best known and most violent draft riots take place in 1863. On July 13, riots break out when the working-class in New York City challenge new legislation to draft men into the Union armies. The violence includes arson, beatings, shootings, and hangings, and lasts until July 16. By the time it ends, some 2,000 people have been injured, 120 killed (including at least two women and eight lynched blacks), and 50 buildings burned to the ground. The riots only end when President Lincoln sends in large numbers of Union soldiers to put them down. Except for the Civil War itself, the mob violence is considered the largest civil and racial insurrection in American history.

The Civil War Ends

Contrary to popular belief, the Civil War does not end all at once, but sputters to a fitful close.

The first major army to surrender is Robert E. Lee's Army of Northern Virginia, which does to to General Ulysses S. Grant at Appomattox Courthouse on April 9, 1865. Joseph E. Johnston capitulates his mixed command in North Carolina that same month on April 26 to General William T. Sherman. Smaller surrenders occur between those dates.

(Facing page) The Wilmer McLean house in Appomattox Courthouse, Virginia. It was here, in the McLean parlor, that General Robert E. Lee formally surrendered his Army of Northern Virginia to Lt. Gen. U. S. Grant on April 9, 1865. After the Battle of First Bull Run was fought on some of his land in northern Virginia, McLean decided to move deeper into the state to avoid the clashing armies. Little did he know the Civil War, at least in Virginia, would end inside his new home. *LOC*

The last major Confederate force to put down its arms is General Edmund Kirby Smith's command in the Trans-Mississippi Theater on May 26, 1865. On June 23, Cherokee leader and Confederate officer Stand Watie is the last Confederate general to surrender his men; he does so in Doaksville in the Choctaw Nation (modern-day Oklahoma). The last formal capitulation is the raider CSS *Shenandoah*, which surrenders in England on November 7, 1865.

The War Department orders a Grand Review in Washington, D.C., to celebrate the Union victory. The armies march for two days (May 23-24, 1865) as spectators line the sidewalks and lean out of windows to watch. This photograph shows General Slocum and staff and the Army of Georgia passing in review. General William Sherman declares the review "a fitting conclusion to the campaign and the war." *LOC*

Union cavalry units fill the street during the Grand Review at Washington, D.C., to celebrate the Federal victory. Bands play and spectators cheer as the horsemen and artillery units move along the main streets. "The whole thing went off quietly & without a blunder," writes one private in his journal at the end of the day. LOC

With the war finally over, the Union army gathers one last time for a final Grand Review in Washington, D.C., that May. Once that ends, more than one million soldiers are on their way home to an uncertain future. They are changed by the war in ways they do not understand. The veterans also bring home a new sense of nation. They have seen more of it than they ever imagined, and it is much larger than any ever dreamed. In many ways they now also share a common view of the future of the United States and will spend another half-century trying to shape it.

Photography

The Civil War is the first conflict extensively documented by photography. An estimated 1,500 photographers work during the conflict. Unfortunately, the vast majority are unknown to us. The most famous is New Yorker Mathew Brady. Another is his assistant, Alexander Gardner.

Ken Burns' early 1990s documentary "The Civil War," which captures the imaginations of people everywhere, is based upon photographs taken (mostly) during the war by Brady and others. Although we have thousands of images today, Burns and others explained that thousands more were lost or destroyed after the war ended. Because they were made from glass plates, for example, large numbers were used in greenhouses, leaving the sun to do its inevitable damage.

The farsighted Brady realizes the approaching war offers a rare opportunity. First and foremost a businessman, he realizes departing soldiers offer a lucrative chance to play on parental heartstrings, and so he runs an ad in a New York paper announcing, "You cannot tell how soon it may be too late." It works. The idea of capturing the war itself intrigues Brady, who asks General Winfield Scott and President Lincoln for permission to go to the battlefields. Lincoln agrees, but only if Brady pays for the trip himself. Brady quickly organizes a corps of photographers to follow the armies.

Producing a photograph in the 1860s is quite a process. Two photographers are usually required to capture a picture. It is especially difficult to work from a photography wagon on a battlefield. One photographer prepares clean glass plates and the chemicals needed, which he pours onto the plate. After some time for the chemicals to evaporate, the plate is immersed in a bath solution and placed in a holder. This process is done in complete darkness.

To use the plate, the photographer inserts the holder into the camera, which is positioned by the other photographer. Exposure of the plate—usually several seconds—and development of the photograph have to be completed

Battlefield photographers use small wagons in which to develop the plates they use. The slow and awkward process requires chemical baths and complete darkness. The most famous photographer of the day is Mathew Brady, but an estimated 1,500 are at work during the Civil War. Confederate photographers are often hampered by a lack of chemicals and other supplies. *LOC*

within minutes. Each exposed plate is rushed to the darkroom wagon for developing. The resulting glass plate negative is very fragile.

In addition to capturing the images of tens of thousands of young men for the folks back home, photographers like Brady and others also do something never before achieved: they photograph the aftermath of a battle and share the gruesome sights with the public back home. Gardner and James Gibson, both of whom works for Brady, photographs the immediate aftermath of the Battle of Antietam fought on September 17, 1862. Nearly everyone in that era still believes war is a noble and romantic venture filled with glory and chivalry. That naive view changes when "death studies" of grotesque bloated dead bodies covered with flies in every conceivable position goes on public exhibit just a month after the battle. Mr. Brady, writes the *The New York Times*, "has done something to bring home to us the terrible reality and earnestness of war. If he has not brought bodies and laid them in our dooryards and along the streets, he has done something very like it."

Confederate dead at Antietam, as photographed by Mathew Brady. It is the first time in history the general public sees images of battlefield dead—and it horrifies them. LOC

The stark black and white photos from more than 150 years ago still evoke a powerful emotional response that makes them memorable. The portrait of Abraham Lincoln taken on April 10, 1865, in a photo studio in Washington, D.C. just one week before his assassination, occurred just one day after General Robert E. Lee surrenders to General U.S. Grant. It was the last photograph Lincoln will sit for.

The battlefield images that so stunned the nation can still cause the heart to catch. Two of the most powerful include Confederate dead lining the Hagerstown Pike at Antietam (above), and the supposed Rebel sharpshooter killed in the Devil's Den at Gettysburg, likely by a shot fired from a Union rifle on Little Round Top. Both remind viewers of the horror and waste of war. As it turns out, the photographer staged the Gettysburg image by moving the body from another place after photographing it there. Staged or not, this and other photographs brought the war in graphic terms to the Union home front in a way that little else could do.

Many more images of Southern dead were taken than Union dead. Photography, after all, was a business. Selling images in the North of dead Union boys was not likely to go over well.

(Top) General William T. Sherman outside Atlanta in Federal fort #7, taken by George N. Barnard, the best-known photographer of events in the Western Theater. (Middle) U. S. Grant in 1863 atop Lookout Mountain, Tennessee, with other Union officers. (Below) President Abraham Lincoln in what is believed to be his last photograph, April 10, 1865. *LOC*

Glossary of Civil War Terms

Abatis: A defensive work consisting of a series of felled trees, their ends sharpened and pointed toward the enemy.

Abolitionist: A person who advocates the abolishment, or ending, of slavery.

Anaconda Plan: General Winfield Scott's strategic plan to quell the rebellion, calling for a blockade of Southern ports and occupation of the Mississippi River—squeezing the Confederate states into submission like a giant snake, or anaconda.

Anti-Slavery: A person who is against the spread of slavery, but not necessarily for its abolition in places where it already exists.

Artillery: A term used to describe large-caliber guns, or cannon, as well as the branch of service that operates such weapons.

Blue Belly: Confederate term—derived from the slang "yellowbelly" or coward—for Union soldiers.

Bohemian Brigade: A name given to the large number of newspaper reporters and artists who cover the Civil War. The name stems from a New York City saloon frequented by newspapermen.

Bounty: Money paid by states and the federal government to entice men to enlist in the Union armed forces. Bounties range from several hundred dollars to more than $700.00.

Bounty Jumper: A person who joins the Union armed forces, collects an enlistment bounty, deserts, and repeats the process. Some bounty jumpers join as many as half-a-dozen units during the course of the war.

Breastwork: A temporary defensive work erected to protect troops from enemy fire; often constructed in haste out of available materials, such earth and felled trees.

Brevet: A temporary or honorary rank, often granted for meritorious service during war, which does not carry the authority or pay of a full rank.

Canister: An artillery projectile consisting of small iron or lead balls packed with sawdust into a tin can, or canister, which scatter upon firing, acting like a shotgun blast. Normally fired against attacking infantry, canister rounds have an effective range of 100 to 400 yards.

Carpetbaggers: Northerners who flocked to the South during Reconstruction in search of financial gain. The term is derived from the carpet bags in which such men carry their belongings.

Caisson: A house-drawn wagon or chest designed to carry ammunition for field artillery.

Chevaux-de-frise: A wooden frame (often a single log) embedded with crossed wooden spikes, pointed toward the enemy. Often used to fill gaps in a defensive line.

Christian Commission: A massive volunteer organization that provides aid to soldiers during the war, from reading material to medical supplies and treatment.

Coehorn: A small portable mortar that fired a 24-pound ball up to a distance of 1,500 yards.

Commutation: The process of drafted men paying a fee (often $300.00) to avoid service.

Contrabands: Term used to describe fugitive slaves who come into Union lines during the war. These ex-slaves are considered contrabands of war by U.S. officials because their labor aid the Southern war effort.

Copperheads: Northern Democrats opposed to the war. Also referred to as "Peace Democrats," they advocate an immediate peace settlement with the Confederacy. Many are imprisoned after Abraham Lincoln suspend the right of *habeas corpus.*

Defilade: A position protected, via natural or manmade barrier, from enemy fire or observation.

Demonstration: A secondary or threatened attack designed to deceive the enemy. Demonstrations are made against a portion of the enemy's line away from the target of the main attack.

Dictator, The: The most famous of several large Union mortars used at Petersburg, Virginia, in 1864. The 13-inch seacoast mortar weighs 17,120 lbs. and can fire a 220-lb. ball a distance of more than two miles.

Earthwork: A defensive work erected to protect troops from enemy fire; often consisting of series of trenches.

Ellet Ram Fleet: Union river steamers with a massive iron prow for ramming and sinking enemy vessels.

Emancipation Proclamation: Presidential order, preliminarily issued September 22, 1862, freeing all slaves in states still in rebellion as of January 1, 1863. Slaves in the border states (Delaware, Kentucky, Maryland, Missouri) are exempted. Paves the way for ex-slaves to enter the U.S. Army and Navy.

Enfield Rifle: English muskets used extensively in the Civil War by both sides. The .577-caliber rifled-muskets are of the pattern of 1853 and equipped with the angular bayonet.

Enfilade: Gunfire directed along an enemy's battle line from a flanking position, producing maximum damage with minimum exposure.

Flank: The end of an army's line in battle, or a type of attack directed at an enemy's flank (i.e., a flanking maneuver).

Furlough: Leave granted enlisted men, often those sick or wounded, to return home for a period of time.

Galvanized Yankees: Confederate prisoners of war who swear allegiance to the United States and join the Union army. The six regiments of Galvanized Yankees raised are sent west to fight Indians.

Grand Army of the Republic: The politically powerful fraternal organization of Union veterans of the war, founded in 1866. Often referred to as the GAR.

Grape Shot: An artillery projectile consisting of a number of iron balls held together by iron plates and rings, largely superceded by the start of the war by canister.

Greybacks: 1. Lice. 2. Union troops' slang term for Confederates, derived from their grey uniforms.

Guerrilla: A term for civilians who engage in warfare, or for the hit-and-run tactics they employe.

Hardtack: A hard wheat biscuit, 3 by 3 inches, issued as rations to troops, who regularly deride it as inedible.

Haversack: A small, durable bag in which soldiers carry personal belongings; often slung over one shoulder.

Invalid Corps: A reserve command established in 1863 consisting of Union soldiers (both on active service or recently discharged) too disabled to serve in combat but capable of performing other light military duties (e.g., provost guard, nursing, cooking, garrison duty). Renamed the Veterans Reserve Corp (VRC) in 1864, over 60,000 men serve in its ranks during the war.

Ironclad: A warship covered (clad) with iron plating; all Civil War ironclads are steam powered.

Legion: A regiment consisting of infantry, cavalry, and artillery companies.

Minie Ball: A cone-shaped lead bullet, designed by and named after Captain Claude-Etienne Minié of the French army, used in rifled muskets. The bullet's hollow base expands upon firing, forcing it into the grooves (or rifling) inside the gun's barrel. As a result, the bullet spins as it exits the barrel, stabilizing it in flight and resulting in increased range and accuracy.

Mortar: A large but short-barreled artillery piece designed to lob explosive shells at a high arc toward enemy positions. Used most often during siege operations. The war's largest mortar, called "The Dictator," sends   200-lb. explosive shells a distance of approximately 2 ½ miles.

Old Abe: The bald eagle mascot of the 8th Wisconsin Infantry. The eagle was carried in 37 battles and skirmishes, including Vicksburg, Mississippi.

Parole: Status of prisoners of war released on their personal assurance that they will not again take up arms until formally exchanged.

Picket: A soldier on guard, often beyond the main lines. A group of pickets, or a picket line, is often employed to guard against a surprise enemy attack.

Pontoon: A low, flat-bottomed wooden boat. Pontoon bridges—dozens to hundreds of pontoons strung together and covered with wooden boards— allow advancing armies to cross various bodies of water in short order.

Prolonge: An 18-foot length of heavy rope wound between two hooks on a gun carriage and kept there for use in moving an unlimbered gun.

Quaker Gun: A log painted to resemble a cannon to fool the enemy. The name apparently stems from the Quakers' religious opposition to war.

Ram: A stream-powered boat with an iron ram attached to its bow, designed to sink enemy ships via collision.

Sanitary Commission: Federal government agency created in 1861 to coordinate the volunteer efforts of women during the war. Female volunteers organize fundraisers, staff hospitals, and sew uniforms, among countless other activities.

Scalawag: A white Southerner who supported Republican efforts during Reconstruction.

Secesh: Shorthand for "secessionist," or a person who advocates the secession of southern states in 1860-1861 or supports the Confederate war effort.

Siege: Military tactic by which an enemy force is surrounded, preventing its re-supply and forcing it into eventual surrender.

Skedaddle: Slang word, often employed by soldiers, referring to a hasty withdrawal or retreat.

Skirmish: Light combat, often entailing an exchange of fire between opposing pickets or other advanced forces.

Sutler: A civilian merchant authorized to sell miscellaneous goods (e.g., tobacco, books, food) to soldiers. Sutlers, in horse-drawn wagons or carts, follow the armies and set up shop when the armies camp.

Torpedo: The name used to describe any one of a variety of exploding mines employed during the war, both on land and at sea.

U.S.C.T.: United States Colored Troops, regiments of the U.S. Army that consisted of African-American soldiers commanded by white officers.

Veterans Reserve Corps: see Invalid Corps.

Zouave: A member of a Union or Confederate regiment patterned after the French Zouaves and distinguished by their colorful uniforms, including baggy trousers and turbans or fezzes.

Gallery of Union Soldiers and Sailors

C ivil War photographs show everything from camps and battlefields to the dead. Still, the most haunting images are often the innocent faces of the tens of thousands of young soldiers who posed for pictures.

Felix Thompson, Co. H, 1st Missouri Cavalry, poses with his pistols and saber. The various companies were often separated for various duties. Company H serves in several battles and minor actions, including Pea Ridge and Prairie Grove in Arkansas. The regiment spent most of its service in the Trans- Mississippi Theater. *LOC*

Pvt. John Ryan of Company H, 2nd Rhode Island Infantry, wears brass shoulder scales. His regiment fires the opening volley at First Bull Run in July 1861 and is still in line at the final scene at Appomattox in April 1865. It is believed early in the war that the brass shoulder scales would deflect sword blows, but the scales quickly disappear as the war progressed. *LOC*

An unidentified soldier in the "First Scotch Regiment," 12th Illinois Infantry, poses in his sack coat and Tam o'Shanter cap in front of painted backdrop showing weapons and an American flag. This photo was taken at Benton Barracks, St. Louis. *LOC*

Unidentified solder (left) in a Vermont uniform, Company H, poses with his bayoneted rifle-musket. Vermont sends more than 34,000 to serve in the Civil War out of a total population of about 350,000 citizens. The state is also the site of the northernmost land action in the Civil War when the community of St. Albans is hit by Confederate raiders. *LOC*

Unidentified soldier in Union uniform with bayoneted rifle musket in front of a painted backdrop showing an American flag and column pedestal. These types of individual photographs use a painted backdrop to suggest an outdoor site. The weapons they pose with are usually props provided by the photographer. *LOC*

This dashing soldier with the stylish hat poses in his Union uniform with a Colt pistol in his belt and saber and carbine by his side. He is not identified. *LOC*

Pvt. Thomas McCreary of Company E, 3rd Kentucky Cavalry. The book he is holding is possibly his personal Bible. The regiment fights for the Union in a divided Kentucky and serves in various operations, including the campaign against Atlanta in 1864. By the time it is all over, the regiment loses 215 men killed or mortally wounded, and another 168 by disease. *LOC*

This unidentified solder is in the Zouave uniform of the 34th Indiana Infantry (known as The Morton Rifles). The 34th Indiana has the distinction of fighting in the last land action of the Civil War at Palmito Ranch in May 1865 in Texas along the banks of the Rio Grande river just east of Brownsville. Pvt. John J. Williams, the last Union soldier killed during the war, falls there. *LOC*

An unidentified soldier (left) wears a Union uniform with a Massachusetts militia shako next to him on the table. The shako, popular early in the war, is a tall, cylindrical military cap, usually with a visor, and sometimes tapered at the top. It is usually adorned with some kind of ornamental plate or badge on the front. *LOC*

An African-American soldier (right) poses in his Union cavalry uniform with his saber. Unfortunately, neither he nor his regiment is identified. There are only a few Union black cavalry regiments formed during the Civil War. He might be a member of the 5th U.S. Colored Cavalry, or perhaps the 5th Massachusetts Colored Cavalry. *LOC*

Pvt. Peter L. Foust (next page), Winchester Greys, Co. C, 19th Indiana Volunteer Infantry. He is mortally wounded in the heavy fighting on July 1, 1863 at Gettysburg. The 19th Indiana is one of the original regiments of the Iron Brigade of the West. The brigade suffers the highest percentage of casualties of any Federal brigade in the Civil War. *Civil War Museum, Kenosha, Wis.*

A New York State enlisted man with a bayoneted musket. He is not identified. New York provided 400,000–460,000, or nearly 21 per cent, of all the men in the state and more than half of those under the age of 30. Of the total enlistments, more than 130,000 are foreign-born, including 20,000 from British North American possessions such as Canada. *LOC*

This unidentified cavalry soldier in a Union uniform wears the Model 1858 dress hat. The hat brass identifies him as a member of Company C, 1st Regiment—but from what state? Regiments generally had 10 companies of 100 men each. The brass letter indicates the company and the brass number the regiment. *LOC*

Pvt. Albert H. Davis of Company K, 6th New Hampshire Infantry, in his uniform with shoulder scales and a Model 1858 dress hat. He holds a Model 1841 Mississippi rifle topped with a sword bayonet, and wears a knapsack, bedroll, canteen, and a haversack. Davis is listed among the killed in action at the battle of Fredericksburg on Dec. 13, 1862. *LOC*

Edwin Chamberlain, Company C, 11th New Hampshire Infantry, in a sergeant's uniform with his guitar. Soldiers on both sides of the Civil War make their own music with personal instruments like this guitar. Brass bands are part of the early regiments, but are soon consolidated into brigade bands. *LOC*

An unidentified African-American sailor in Union uniform sits with his arm on a table. At the onset of the Civil War, free black men rush to volunteer for service with the Union forces, but are at first refused because a 1792 law bars them from bearing arms in the U.S. Army. This changes as the war progressed. *LOC*

George Wingate Weeks of Company D, 8th Maine Infantry with his drum in front of painted backdrop showing a shoreline with a house and lighthouse. Drums are used in infantry regiments to control movements and to direct firing. Regiments early in the war include a fife and drum corps under the command of a drum major. *LOC*

African-American soldier in Union Zouave uniform. He is not identified. The name Zouave comes from the regiments in French Army and their colorful garb before the Civil War. In the United States, Zouaves come to public attention because of Elmer E. Ellsworth, who directs the "Zouave Cadets" of Chicago. Zouave-style units serve on both sides in 1861- 1865. *LOC*

This Union sailor poses with an American flag in front of a backdrop showing a naval scene. He is not identified. At the start of the war, the Union Navy had 42 ships in commission. Another 48 are listed as available for service as soon as crews can be assembled and trained to man them. By the end of the war, the Union Navy has 671 active vessels. *LOC*

A Union soldier wears a medal. He is not identified. General Joe Hooker institutes the use of corps badges so a unit can be identified at a distance, and to instill pride and increase morale within the ranks. Each Union army corps has a distinctive shape and each division a variation of the corps badge in a different color. For example, the First Division, First Corps of the Army of the Potomac was a red sphere. *LOC*

An unidentified African-American soldier poses in his Union uniform. In the Union army, more than 179,000 black men will serve in more than 160 units, not counting those who serve in the navy and in various support positions. This number includes both Northern free blacks and former slaves. *LOC*

Pvt. Frederick Lythson, Randall Guards, Company G, 2nd Wisconsin Infantry, Iron Brigade, wears an early grey Wisconsin militia uniform. Lythson is shot through the legs at Gettysburg and transfers to the Veteran Reserve Corps in 1864. An unconfirmed report claims he was killed by Indians out West after the war. *Author*

Unidentified soldier in Union uniform, Zouave fez, and New York buckle, with cap box, musket, and U.S. Model 1862 Zouave sword bayonet in front of a painted backdrop. By the end of the war in 1865, New York provides the Union Army with 27 regiments of cavalry, 15 regiments of artillery, and 248 regiments of infantry. *LOC*

A soldier from Company A, 12th Michigan Infantry poses holding a Lorenz rifle. He is not identified. The Austrian Lorenz was the second most common imported shoulder arm used by both sides during the Civil War. The Union purchases 226,924 and the Confederacy as many as 100,000. *LOC*

Pvt. Hiram M. Kersey, 44th Iowa Infantry, with bayonet, knife, revolver and cartridge box. His regiment is one of the 100-day units organized by various states in 1864 to allow the release of other veteran regiments from less important duties, including guard postings in occupied areas. *LOC*

A Union drummer boy wearing a Zouave uniform. He is not identified. Drummer boys are often depicted in post-Civil War artwork and literature. Because of their young age and considered bravery, they are held up as heroes during the war. The image endures in popular imagination for generations. *LOC*

Brothers Hiram J. and William H. Gripman, Company I, 3rd Minnesota Infantry. Both survive the Civil War. Their regiment is captured near Murfreesboro, Tennessee. After being paroled, the members of the 3rd Minnesota return to their home state, where they take part to help suppress an Indian uprising, and are then sent south to serve in the siege of Vicksburg, Mississippi. *LOC*

Soldier of the 56th New York Volunteers (10th Legion) with musket and sword. He is not identified. New York was the most populous state in the Union during the Civil War, and the state provides more troops to serve in the Union Army than any other state. Many significant and capable military officers also come out of New York, including cavalrymen Tom Devins and Wesley Merritt, and infantry generals James Ricketts and Dan Sickles. *LOC*

Pvt. Jacob Harker, Company G, 120th Ohio Infantry. His regiment serves at Port Gibson and Vicksburg, and suffers a large number of casualties during the Red River Campaign in Louisiana. The survivors form only three companies, and the unit is consolidated with the 114th Ohio in November 1864. Pvt. Harker survives the war. *LOC*

A soldier of the 1st Michigan Engineers and Mechanics holds a Model 1858 Hardee hat with the engineer castle insignia. He is not identified. The Michigan unit is one of three engineering regiments raised in 1861, the other two being from Missouri (August 1861) and New York (September 1861). *LOC*

Numbers and Losses

Numbers are fascinating, and this is especially true in the American Civil War, during which millions of men serve on both sides of the conflict.

The numbers that follow in the table below illustrate everything from the population of both warring sides to the killed, wounded, captured, missing, surrendered— and much more. They tell a dramatic story, and demonstrate at a glance why winning the war would have been extraordinarily difficult for the Confederacy.

NUMBERS AND LOSSES		
	UNION	**CONFEDERACY**
Population	22,400,000	9,103,000
Population of Military Age (18-45)	4,600,000	985,000
TOTAL ENLISTMENTS	2,778,326	1,003,600
Army	2,677,119	1,000,000
Navy	101,207	3,000
Marines	3,000	600
TOTAL DEATHS	359,528	219,000
Killed in Battle	67,088	53,0000
Mortally Wounded	43,012	37,000
Died of Disease	224,586	120,000

Killed in Accidents	4,114	3,000
Drowned	4,944	3,500
Died of Other Known Causes	3,663	2,500
Died of Unknown Causes	12,121	[...]
Died while a Prisoner of War	25,971	27,000
Wounded in Action (not mortally)	275,000	226,000
Captured	211,400	462,000
Deserted	199,000	104,000
Discharged	426,500	57,800
Surrendered in 1865		174,223

After the war, some shocking statistics are reached. It is determined that one of every six Union soldiers was wounded in battle, and one out of every 10 soldiers was captured by the enemy. One of every 13 soldiers died of disease, and one out of every 38 soldiers died from his wounds. The odds of being killed in action were one out of every 48 soldiers.

Glorious Remembrance

The great armies that saved the Union fade away in just a few weeks at the end of the war. The one-time soldiers return to various pursuits of civilian life. They face an uncertain future. They are changed by the war in ways they do not understand.

Tens of thousands of men return to farms and hometowns and large cities missing an arm or leg. Some are carrying diseases of which they are unaware. Even more of the veterans are troubled in mind and spirit by what they have seen and done. Home is also a different place. Wives, younger sisters and brothers, and aging fathers and mothers have been tending crops and livestock and running shops and businesses. In some cases the family members of Union veterans find it hard to step aside for the returning soldiers. Uneasy and restless, many of the soldiers make plans to head West to make new lives. Nothing is ever going to be quite the same again.

The veterans also bring home a new sense of nation. They have seen the country and marched over it. They share a common view of the future of the United States and will spend the rest of their lives trying to shape it. In many ways, the American Civil War is never going to end. The issues that caused the conflict of 1861 to 1865 will still be debated more than 150 years afterward—the civil rights of individuals, what it means to be an American citizen, the rights of states in a strong central government, and the role of the president in times of war.

In so many ways, the nation will always be working on what President Lincoln in his little speech at Gettysburg calls "a new birth of freedom." His words will always remind the veterans as they go about their lives in a world of growing complexity that freedom is bought with sacrifice, hard work, and understanding.

At first, the veterans—still young men—turn aside thoughts of the war and what it cost. They have little time for reunions or military matters. Attempts to organize such meetings of old soldiers are failures or meet modest success. Dr. Benjamin F. Stephenson, former surgeon of the 14th Illinois Infantry, is one of the first calling for a veteran's organization, and after the war he is among several individuals pushing such an effort. How the label Grand Army of the Republic came to be is unknown, but it is a mighty name.

A call for a special "Decoration or Memorial Day" each May by former Gen. John A. Logan of Illinois, then president of the GAR, to decorate the graves of fallen soldiers is met with favor. Following an initial period of enthusiasm, however, the GAR experiences waning interest by the Union veterans. Then comes a grand resurgence that brings national encampments, huge parades and the dedication of thousands of monuments to mark the soldiers' service.

"We were too occupied building lives and families and businesses that had been neglected by our years in uniform," one veteran explains. "Then one day we looked up from our work and saw dimming eyes and graying hair. Suddenly we wanted to talk again with our old comrades and of our soldier days when we were young,"

And then, one day in the middle of the twentieth century, the last of them died, and the Boys in Blue were just a memory.

The Memorial Day Order

Headquarters Grand Army of the Republic. Adjutant Generals' office No 444, 14th Street Washington, D.C. May 5th 1868

General Orders No.11.

I. The 30th day of May 1868 is designated for the purpose of strewing with flowers or otherwise decorating the graves of comrades, who died in defense, of their country during the late rebellion, and whose bodies now lie in almost every City, Village, and hamlet, church yard in the land. In this observance no form of ceremony is prescribed, but Posts and comrades will in their own way arrange such fitting services and testimonials of respect as circumstances may permit. . .

II. It is the purpose of the commander in chief to inaugurate this observance with the hope that it will be kept up from year, to year, while a survivor of the war remains, to honor the memory of his departed comrades. He earnestly desires the public press to call attention to this order, and lend its friendly aid in bringing it to the notice of comrades in all parts of the country in time for simultaneous compliance therewith.

III. Department commanders will use every effort to make this order effective.

By order of John A. Logan, Commander in Chief

Official A. P. Chipman Adjutant General

The Last Soldier Grave at Gettysburg

A military color guard, the playing of "Taps," and a fired salute marks the burial on July 1, 1997, of the last soldier found on the battlefield of Gettysburg.

The body is discovered in a washout on the famous Railroad Cut northwest of town in 1996. This is the same area where the Iron Brigade of the Army of the Potomac—made up of three regiments from Wisconsin, one from Michigan, and one from Indiana—is heavily engaged on July 1, 1863. The soldier is in his 20s and died from a gunshot wound to the head. It can not be determined whether he is Union or Confederate. He is buried in the unknown section of the Soldiers' National Cemetery at Gettysburg.

A modern view of the famous Railroad Cut, where so many fought and died. *Author*

Researching your Union Ancestor

Do you have an ancestor who was a Union soldier in the Civil War? Some 2,100,000 men were mustered into the Union army during the four years of fighting, including black Americans and Native Americans. Perhaps your ancestor is a great-great-great grandmother or aunt who served as a nurse or spy. The Civil War touched almost every Northern citizen during its four years. If you are interested in finding out about your family history, there are ways to find ancestors who served in the 1861-1865 era.

Civil War records are scattered in various federal, state, and local repositories. Your ancestor's military career, physical description, and occupation can be found, but you must first know the soldier's unit in which he fought. A good place to start is the Soldiers and Sailors Data site: www.nps.gov/civilwar/soldiers-and-sailors-database.htm.

At the search portal, enter a name and state, and some basic information pops up so you can carry your search further, such as looking at state or census records. Another source of information on individuals is the National Archives: www.archives.gov/research. There, you can find pension files and compiled military service records.

In addition to checking with various state or local archives, also check various lineage societies, such as the Sons of the Union Veterans of the Civil War: www.suvcw.org/; and the Church of Latter Day Saints genealogy site: www.familysearch.org.

For other digitized records, visit your public library or subscription-based web sites like www.ancestry.com.

Once you have located an ancestor in the Soldiers and Sailors Database you can use military rosters, veterans' rosters, and pension records to find more about an individual soldier and the details of his service. These sources are usually available in the holdings of state achieves.

After you identify the regiment (the basic 1,000-man unit of Civil War armies) and which company (the 100-man basic unit of a regiment), you can begin the task of finding out where and when he served. Many states have detailed records of individual soldiers, including his appearance, former occupation, and where he enlisted.

Also look at sources for the war on a larger scale, such as unit histories and material on battles, campaigns, and generals. One of the main sources of information is the multi-volume *Official Records of the War of Rebellion* published after the war. It has an extensive index.

Not to be neglected are the visual records of regiments and individuals. These include the small individual pictures that might be available, as well as photographs of his regiment. They can provide more clues and add to your understanding of the war.

The Federal census and city directories, as well as local histories and local newspapers, can also be helpful. Newspapers are a rich and often overlooked source for information.

Many stories still need to be discovered, and the search can be as rewarding as the actual discovery of material on you ancestor.

Good hunting.

Civil War Points of Interest

Whether searching for a Civil War related locale in your area or planning an extended Civil War themed trip, the following list of sites will get you started. All contact information—including websites, where available—was current at the time of publication. Operating hours vary, so please check ahead before hitting the road.

*   *   *

Alabama

Confederate Memorial Park
437 County Road 63
Marbury, Alabama 36051
(205) 755-1990
groups.msn.com/AutaugaatWar/confederatememorialpark.msnw
Two cemeteries and a museum tell the story of Alabama's Confederate Soldiers' Home.

Fort Gaines Historical Site
51 Bienville Boulevard
Dauphin Island, Alabama 36528
(251) 861-6992
www.dauphinisland.org/fort.htm
Fort Gaines protected Mobile Bay from Union attack during the Civil War.

Fort Morgan State Historic Site
51 Highway 180 West
Gulf Shores, Alabama 36542
(334) 540-7125
Visitors can view the bay through which Admiral David Farragut's fleet passed during the Battle of Mobile Bay.

Arkansas

Arkansas Post National Memorial
1741 Old Post Road
Gillett, Arkansas 72055
870-548-2207
www.nps.gov/arpo/index.htm
Preserves the site of Fort Hindman, constructed by Confederates in 1862 and captured by Federal forces in 1863. The earthen structure has since been destroyed by erosion.

Jenkins Ferry State Park
Located 13 miles south of Sheridan on Ark. 46
www.arkansasstateparks.com/park-finder/parks.aspx?id=28
(No staff on site.)
Federal troops retreating after the failed Red River campaign beat off Confederate attacks and crossed the Saline River here on April 30, 1864.

Marks' Mills State Park
Located southeast of Fordyce at the junction of Ark. 97 and Ark. 8
888-AT-PARKS
www.arkansasstateparks.com/marksmills/
During the Red River campaign in April 1864, Confederates captured a 220-wagon Union supply train here.

Pea Ridge National Military Park
15930 E Highway 62
Garfield, Arkansas 72732
(479) 451-8122
www.nps.gov/peri/
Several thousand Native Americans fought with the Confederate army at Elkhorn Tavern (Pea Ridge). U.S. forces won the battle, keeping Missouri in the Union.

Poison Spring State Park
Located 10 miles west of Camden on Ark. 76
888-AT-PARKS
www.arkansasstateparks.com/poisonspring/
A Red River Campaign spot at which Confederates ambushed a Union supply train, capturing 198 wagons loaded with corn.

Prairie Grove Battlefield State Park
506 East Douglas Street
Prairie Grove, Arkansas 72753
(479) 846-2990
www.arkansasstateparks.com/prairiegrovebattlefield/
This December 1862 battle was the last major engagement fought in northeastern Arkansas.

Colorado

Sand Creek Massacre National Historic Site
35110 Highway 194 E.
La Junta, Colorado 81050
(719) 438-5916
www.nps.gov/sand/index.htm
In late November 1864, soldiers under Col. John Chivington attacked Cheyenne Chief Black Kettle's village.

District of Columbia

Ford's Theatre National Historical Park
511 10th Street NW
Washington, D.C. 20004
(202) 233-0701
www.nps.gov/foth/
John Wilkes Booth assassinated Abraham Lincoln here on April 14, 1865.
The president died the next morning, across the street in the Petersen House.

Fort Circle Parks
Located at various sites in and around the city
www.nps.gov/cwdw/index.htm
Visitors can view the locations and remnants of a number of the forts
erected to defend the capital during the war.

Lincoln's Cottage at the Soldiers' Home
140 Rock Creek Church Road NW
Washington, D.C. 20011
(202) 829-0436
www.lincolncottage.org/index.htm
Lincoln and his family lived here for long stretches of time during the war.

Florida

Gulf Islands National Seashore - Gulf Breeze
1801 Gulf Breeze Parkway
Gulf Breeze, Florida 32563
(850) 934-2600
www.nps.gov/guis/index.htm
Civil War-era Forts Barrancas, Pickens, Massachusetts, and McRee are
located within the park.

Natural Bridge Battlefield Historic State Park
7502 Natural Bridge Road

Tallahassee, Florida 32305
(850) 922-6007
www.floridastateparks.org/naturalbridge/default.cfm
Confederates turned back a Federal advance here on March 6, 1865.

Olustee Battlefield Historic State Park
P.O. Box 40
Olustee, Florida 32072
(386) 758-0400
www.floridastateparks.org/olustee/default.cfm
Site of the February 1864 battle in which several U.S. Colored Troops regiments participated.

Georgia

Andersonville National Historic Site
496 Cemetery Road
Andersonville, Georgia 31711
(229) 924-0343
www.nps.gov/ande/
Site of the largest Confederate-run POW camp, at which over 12,000 Union soldiers perished.

Chickamauga and Chattanooga National Military Park
P.O. Box 2128
Fort Oglethorpe, Georgia 30742
(706) 866-9241
www.nps.gov/chch/
The nation's first national military park preserves the site of the only major Confederate victory of the war in the Western Theater, one of the largest battles of the entire war.

Fort McAllister Historic Park
3894 Fort McAllister Road
Richmond Hill, Georgia 31324
(912) 727-2339
gastateparks.org/info/ftmcallister/
The Confederate garrison at Fort McAllister, located south of Savannah, beat off seven attacks by enemy warships before falling to Union ground forces in 1864.

Fort Pulaski National Monument — Tybee Island
P.O. Box 30757
Savannah, Georgia 31410
(912) 786-5787
www.nps.gov/fopu/
Considered invincible, Fort Pulaski guarded the water approach to Savannah. In April 1862, U.S. rifled cannon battered the fort into submission in less than two days.

Jefferson Davis Memorial Historic Site
338 Jeff Davis Park Road
Fitzgerald, Georgia 31750
(229) 831-2335
A monument and museum mark the site were Union forces captured the Confederate president on May 9, 1865.

Kennesaw Mountain National Battlefield Park
900 Kennesaw Mountain Drive
Kennesaw, Georgia 30152
(770) 427-4686
www.nps.gov/kemo/
At Kennesaw Mountain, Confederates foiled General William T. Sherman's attempt to break their lines during the campaign for Atlanta.

Pickett's Mill Battlefield Historic Site
4432 Mt. Tabor Church Road
Dallas, Georgia 30157
(770) 443-7850
www.gastateparks.org/info/picketts/
This site of a May 27, 1864, Confederate victory, is one of the few preserved battlefields near Atlanta.

Illinois

Lincoln Home National Historic Site
413 South Eighth Street
Springfield, Illinois 62701-1905
(217) 391-3226
www.nps.gov/liho/
President Lincoln lived here from 1844 until he left for Washington in 1861.

Indiana

Lincoln Boyhood National Memorial
2916 E. South Street
Lincoln City, Indiana 47552
(812) 937-4541
www.nps.gov/libo/
An interpretive site devoted to Lincoln's formative years in Indiana.

Kansas

Fort Scott National Historic Site
P.O. Box 918
Fort Scott, Kansas 66701
(620) 223-0310
www.nps.gov/libo/
Fort Scott served as a Union supply depot during the war.

John Brown State Historic Site
10th and Main Street
Osawatomie, Kansas
(913) 755-4384
www.kshs.org/places/johnbrown/index.htm
View the cabin where abolitionist John Brown fought pro-slavery militia in 1856.

Mine Creek Battlefield State Historic Site
20485 Kansas Highway 52
Pleasanton Kansas 66075
(913) 352-8890
www.kshs.org/places/minecreek/index.htm
On October 25, 1864, outnumbered Union cavalry defeated their counterparts at Mine Creek, capturing roughly 600 Confederates, including two generals.

Marais des Cygnes State Historic Site
20485 Kansas Highway 52
Pleasanton Kansas 66075
(913) 352-8890
www.kshs.org/places/marais/index.htm
Visitors can tour the site of the murder of five free-state settlers by pro-slavery settlers during the "Bleeding Kansas" era.

Kentucky

Abraham Lincoln Birthplace National Historic Site
2995 Lincoln Farm Road
Hodgenville, Kentucky 42748
(270) 358-3137
www.nps.gov/abli/index.htm
Abraham Lincoln was born here on February 12, 1809.

Columbus-Belmont State Park
350 Park Road
Columbus, Kentucky 42032
(270) 677-2327
parks.ky.gov/findparks/recparks/cb/
U.S. Grant, in his first battle as a Union general, defeated Confederates at Belmont in November 1861.

Jefferson Davis Monument State Historic Site
Highway 68 E
Fairview, Kentucky 42221
(270) 889-6100
parks.ky.gov/findparks/histparks/jd/
Jefferson Davis was born here on June 3, 1808.

Perryville Battlefield State Historic Site
1825 Battlefield Road
Perryville, Kentucky 40468-0296
859-332-8631
parks.ky.gov/findparks/histparks/pb/
The decisive Battle of Perryville ended Braxton Bragg's 1862 invasion of Kentucky, keeping the state in the Union.

Louisiana

Camp Moore Confederate Cemetery and Museum
Hwy. 51
Tangipahoa, Louisiana
(985) 229-2438
personal.atl.bellsouth.net/c/o/cosby_w/
Camp Moore was Louisiana's largest Civil War training camp.

Centenary State Historic Site
3522 College St.
Jackson, Louisiana 70748
(225) 634-7925
crt.state.la.us/parks/icentenary.aspx
Centenary College closed during the war, and both sides utilized its vacant buildings (as hospital space and headquarters).

Fort Pike State Historic Site
27100 Chef Menteur Highway
New Orleans, Louisiana 70129
(504) 255-9171
www.crt.state.la.us/parks/iFortpike.aspx
Confederates occupied Fort Pike at the onset of the war, but abandoned it when Federal troops took New Orleans. Under Union control, the fort became a training ground for members of U.S.C.T. regiments.

Mansfield State Historic Site – Mansfield
15149 Highway 175
Mansfield, Louisiana 71052
(318) 872-1474
www.crt.state.la.us/parks/iMansfld.aspx
The Confederate victory at Mansfield halted Nathaniel P. Banks's Red River Expedition.

Port Hudson State Historic Site - Jackson
236 Hwy 61
Jackson, Louisiana 70748
(225) 654-3775
www.crt.state.la.us/parks/ipthudson.aspx
Port Hudson, the last Confederate stronghold on the Mississippi River, surrendered after a 48-day siege.

Maryland

Antietam National Battlefield
P.O. Box 158
Sharpsburg, Maryland 21782
(301) 432-5124
www.nps.gov/anti/
The Battle of Antietam, the bloodiest single-day battle of the war, marked the end of Robert E. lee's first invasion of the North.

Clara Barton National Historic Site
5801 Oxford Road
Glen Echo, Maryland 20812
(301) 320-1410
www.nps.gov/clba/
Visitors can tour the home of Clara Barton, Civil War nurse and founder of the American Red Cross.

Fort Washington Park
13551 Fort Washington Road
Fort Washington, Maryland 20744
(301) 763-4600
www.nps.gov/fowa/index.htm
Fort Washington was one the many structures that guarded Washington D.C., during the war.

Gathland State Park
21843 National Pike
Boonsboro, Maryland 21713
(301) 791-4767
www.dnr.state.md.us/publiclands/western/gathland.html
The park protects much of the site of the 1862 fight for South Mountain, a precursor to the Battle of Antietam.

Monocacy National Battlefield
5201 Urbana Pike
Frederick, Maryland 21704
(301) 662-3515
www.nps.gov/mono/
The engagement at Monocacy, known as "the battle that saved Washington," occurred during Confederate General Jubal Early's advance toward the capital in the summer of 1864.

National Museum of Civil War Medicine
48 E. Patrick Street
Frederick, Maryland 21705-0470
301-695-1864
www.civilwarmed.org/
Visitors interested in the medical side of the war will enjoy the museum's many programs and exhibits.

Michigan

Historic Fort Wayne
6325 W. Jefferson Ave.
Detroit, Michigan 438209
(313) 628-0796
www.historicfortwaynecoalition.com/
This fort was established in 1845 and used as a place of induction to the U.S. military service.

Minnesota

Historic Fort Snelling
200 Tower Avenue
St. Paul, Minnesota 55111
(612)-725-1171
www.historicfortsnelling.org/
The fort was established in 1819 by Col. Josiah Snelling and his troops, who opened the area to homesteaders.

Wood Lake Battlefield
Granite Falls, Minnesota 56241
(507)-280-9970
www.woodlakebattlefield.com/
Site of a major engagement during the U.S.-Dakota war in 1862 when Minnesota had its own civil war within the larger Civil War.

Fort Ridgely
82404 County Road 30
Fairfax, MN 55332
(507) 426-7888 or 507-934-2160
www.dnr.state.mn.us/state_parks/fort_ridgely/
Built in 1853 as a police station to keep peace as settlers poured into former Dakota lands, it withstood several attacks in the U.S.-Dakota War of 1862 and became a training ground for Civil War recruits.

Mississippi

Beauvoir—The Jefferson Davis Home and Presidential Library
2244 Beach Blvd.
Biloxi, Mississippi 39531
(228) 388-4400
www.beauvoir.org/
Davis's final residence was used as a Confederate Veterans Home between 1903 and 1957.

Brices Cross Roads National Battlefield Site
Located on Mississippi 370 near Baldwyn, Mississippi.
http://www.nps.gov/brcr/
(No visitor center.) For more information, contact:
Natchez Trace Parkway Visitor Center (800) 305-7417
On June 10, 1864, Major General Nathan Bedford Forrest's 3,500-man cavalry corps routed General Samuel D. Sturgis's 8,100 Union troops.

Grand Gulf Military Park
12006 Grand Gulf Road
Port Gibson, Mississippi 39150
(601) 437-5911
www.grandgulfpark.state.ms.us/
The Confederate battery at Grand Gulf drove off Rear Admiral David D. Porter's ironclads, thwarting U.S. Grant's plans to land troops there.

Tupelo National Battlefield
Located on Main Street in Tupelo, Mississippi.
www.nps.gov/tupe/
(No visitor center.)
For more information, contact: Natchez Trace Parkway Visitor Center
(800) 305-7417
Federal troops beat back multiple Confederate attacks during this 1864 battle.

Vicksburg National Military Park
3201 Clay Street
Vicksburg, Mississippi 39183-3495
(601) 636-0583
www.nps.gov/vick/
U.S. Grant's siege and capture of Vicksburg helped split the Confederacy in two, opening the Mississippi River to Union shipping.

Missouri

Battle of Athens State Historic Site
Route 1, Box 26, Hwy CC
Revere, Missouri 63465
(660) 877-3871
www.mostateparks.com/athens.htm
The site of the northernmost Civil War battle fought west of the Mississippi.

Battle of Lexington State Historic Site
101 Delaware Street
Lexington, Missouri 64067
(660) 259-4654
www.mostateparks.com/lexington/index.html
The restored Anderson House still shows damage inflicted by cannon balls fired during the "Battle of the Hemp Bales."

Confederate Memorial State Historic Site
211 West First Street
Higginsville, Missouri 64037
(660) 584-2853
www.mostateparks.com/confedmem.htm
Although Missouri remained in the Union, many of its residents fought for the Confederacy. The Confederate Soldiers Home of Missouri opened in 1891 and housed over 1,600 Confederate veterans and their families during almost 60 years of operation.

Ulysses S Grant National Historic Site
7400 Grant Road
St. Louis, Missouri 63123
(314) 842-3298
www.nps.gov/ulsg/
Visitors can tour "White Haven," the childhood home of Gant's wife, Julia Dent, where the couple lived in the 1850s.

Wilson's Creek National Battlefield
6424 West Farm Road 182
Republic, Missouri 65738
(417) 732-2662
www.nps.gov/wicr/
The Confederates won this 1861 battle, in which Union General Nathaniel Lyon met his death.

New Mexico

Pecos National Historical Park
P.O. Box 418
Pecos, New Mexico 87552-0418
(505) 757-7200
www.nps.gov/peco/
The 1862 Battle of Glorieta Pass marked the end of Confederate occupation of New Mexico.

North Carolina

Bennett Place
4409 Bennett Memorial Road
Durham, North Carolina 27705
(919) 383-4345
www.nchistoricsites.org/Bennett/Bennett.htm
This restored farmhouse was the site of the surrender of General Joseph Johnston's Confederate army.

Bentonville Battlefield
5466 Harper House Road
Four Oaks, North Carolina 27524
(910) 594-0789
www.nchistoricsites.org/Bentonvi/Bentonvi.HTM
Bentonville represented the final Confederate attempt to stop Sherman's advance through North Carolina. Visitors may tour the 1850s Harper House, which was used as a field hospital after the battle.

CSS Neuse State Historic Site
2612 W. Vernon Avenue
Kinston, North Carolina 28502
(252) 522-2091
nchistoricsites.org/neuse/neuse.htm
Displays remnants of the salvaged ironclad gunboat CSS *Neuse.*

Fort Fisher
P.O. Box 169
Kure Beach, North Carolina 28449
(910) 458-5538
www.nchistoricsites.org/fisher/fisher.htm
Fort Fisher fell on January 15, 1865, closing the Confederacy's largest
remaining port, Wilmington, North Carolina.

Fort Macon State Park
2300 East Fort Macon Road
Atlantic Beach, North Carolina 28512
(252) 726-3775
www.ncparks.gov/Visit/parks/foma/main.php
Confederates seized the fort in 1861; Union troops took it back in 1862.

Pennsylvania

Gettysburg National Military Park
1195 Baltimore Pike
Gettysburg, Pennsylvania 17325
(717) 334-1124
www.nps.gov/gett/
The sprawling field covers much of the three-day battle at Gettysburg,
which ended Robert E. Lee's second invasion of the North.

National Civil War Museum
One Lincoln Circle at Reservoir Park
P.O. Box 1861
Harrisburg, Pennsylvania 17105-1861
(717) 260-1861
www.nationalcivilwarmuseum.org/
A variety of exhibits tell the story of the war.

South Carolina

Fort Sumter National Mounument
340 Concord Street
Charleston, South Carolina
www.nps.gov/fosu
The visitor education center's extensive collections shed light on the causes of the war and its outbreak at Fort Sumter in April 1861. The fort itself is a separate entity; those wishing to visit it must do so by ferry. For more information, see the Fort Sumter National Monument's website (link above).

Rivers Bridge State Historic Site
325 State Park Road
Ehrhardt, South Carolina 29081
(803) 267-3675
www.southcarolinaparks.com/park-finder/state-park/566.aspx
For two days in early February 1865, outnumbered Confederates slowed Sherman's march through South Carolina at Rivers Bridge.

Tennessee

Carnton Plantation
1345 Carnton Lane
Franklin, Tennessee 37064
(615) 794-0903
www.carnton.org/
The November 1864 Battle of Franklin swirled about John McGavock's plantation home, which afterward served as a field hospital. After the war, the McGavock family put aside land to serve as a cemetery, in which some 1,500 Confederates are buried.

Carter House
1140 Columbia Ave
Franklin, Tennessee 37065
(615) 791-1861

www.carterhouse1864.com/

This state-owned site preserves the location of Confederate General John B. Hood's disastrous attack on General John M. Schofield's Union army at Franklin. Confederate Captain Theodrick Carter, mortally wounded in the attack, died two days later at his family's home, the Carter House.

Chickamauga and Chattanooga National Military Park – Lookout Mountain Unit (See entry under Georgia for contact information.)

After defeating William S. Rosecrans's Federals at Chickamauga, Confederate General Braxton Bragg laid siege to Chattanooga. Grant replaced Rosecrans and soon drove Bragg's army from its positions.

Fort Donelson National Battlefield
P.O. Box 434
Dover, Tennessee 37058
(931) 232-5348
nps.gov/fodo/index.htm

When Fort Donelson's Confederate commander asked Union General U.S. Grant for surrender terms, Grant replied: "No terms except an unconditional and immediate surrender can be accepted." The loss of Donelson opened Tennessee to invasion by Federal troops.

Fort Pillow State Historic Park
3122 Park Road
Henning, Tennessee 38041
(731) 738-5581
www.tennessee.gov/environment/parks/FortPillow/

On April 12, 1864, Major General Nathan Bedford Forrest's Confederates overran the Union fort, killing 350 troops, many of them black, in an event widely regarded as a massacre.

Johnsonville State Historic Park
90 Redoubt Lane
New Johnsonville, Tennessee 37134

(931) 535-2789
www.tennessee.gov/environment/parks/Johnsonville/
On November 4, 1864, Nathan Bedford Forrest's Confederate cavalry raided Johnsonville, capturing four Union gunboats and 14 steamboats.

Shiloh National Military Park
1055 Pittsburg Landing Road
Shiloh, Tennessee 38376
(731) 689-5696
www.nps.gov/shil/
A Union victory, the two-day battle at Shiloh witnessed the death of the Confederate commander, Albert Sidney Johnston.

Stones River National Battlefield
3501 Old Nashville Highway
Murfreesboro, Tennessee 37129
(615) 893-9501
www.nps.gov/stri/
The Federal victory at Stones River drove Braxton Bragg's Confederate army from its winter quarters.

Texas

Sabine Pass Battleground State Historic Site
6100 Dowling Road
Port Arthur, Texas 77640
(512) 463-6323
www.thc.state.tx.us/hsites/hs_sabine.aspx?Site=Sabine
A bronze statue of Lieutenant Dick Dowling marks the site where he and his 46 Confederates drove off four Union gunboats and seven troop transports, saving East Texas from invasion.

Virginia

American Civil War Museum
1201 E. Clay Street
Richmond, Virginia 23219
(804) 649-1861
www.moc.org/site/PageServer/
The museum holds one of the largest collections of Confederate artifacts in the country and the White House of the Confederacy.

Appomattox Court House National Historical Park
P.O. Box 218
Appomattox, Virginia 24522
(434) 352-8987
www.nps.gov/apco/index.htm
Visitors to the park can view the reconstructed McLean House, where Robert E. Lee surrendered to U.S. Grant in April 1865.

Arlington House, The Robert E. Lee Memorial
Arlington National Cemetery
(703) 235-1530
www.nps.gov/arho/index.htm
Arlington was Robert E. Lee's home for over 30 years. In 1861, the Lees fled south, never to return.

Cedar Creek & Belle Grove National Historical Park – Middletown and Strasburg
7712 Main Street
Middletown, Virginia 22645
(540) 869-30151
www.nps.gov/cebe/index.htm

Fredericksburg & Spotsylvania National Military Park
120 Chatham Lane

Fredericksburg, Virginia 22405
This remarkable park covers several battles, including Fredericksburg, Spotsylvania, Chancellorsville, and smaller engagements.

Manassas National Battlefield Park
12521 Lee Highway
Manassas, Virginia 20109-2005
(703) 361-1339
www.nps.gov/mana/index.htm
The Confederates won the first Battle of Manassas in 1861. A year later, the armies met on the same ground, and the Confederates again prevailed.

Petersburg National Battlefield
1539 Hickory Hill Road
Petersburg, VA 23803
(804) 732-3531
www.nps.gov/pete/index.htm
The 292-day Union siege of Petersburg cost some 20,000 Confederates their lives.

Richmond National Battlefield Park
3215 East Broad Street
Richmond, VA 23223
(804) 226-1981
www.nps.gov/rich/index.htm
Visitors can tour sites from both the 1862 and 1864 Union attempts to capture Richmond, the capital of the Confederacy.

Sailor's Creek Battlefield State Park
6541 Saylers Creek Road
Rice, Virginia 23966
(804) 561-7510
www.dcr.virginia.gov/state_parks/sai.shtml

Philip Sheridan's Union cavalry cut off about one-fourth of Lee's retreating army here in April 1865. Over 7,700 Confederates surrendered, including eight generals.

Staunton River Bridge
The park has two visitor centers.
Call (434) 454-4312 for directions.
www.stauntonriverbattlefield.org/
On June 25, 1864, 492 old men and young boys helped 296 Confederate reserves defeat over 5,000 Union cavalrymen.

West Virginia

Carnifex Ferry Battlefield State Park
1194 Carnifex Ferry Road
Summersville, West Virginia 26651
(304) 872-0825
www.carnifexferrybattlefieldstatepark.com/
Union forces retained control of the Kanawha Valley after their victory in this 1861 battle.

Droop Mountain Battlefield State Park
HC 64 Box 189
Hillsboro, West Virginia 24946
www.droopmountainbattlefield.com/
The Union victory at Droop Mountain ended Confederate operations in West Virginia.

Harpers Ferry National Historical Park
P.O. Box 65
Harpers Ferry, West Virginia 25425
(304) 535-6029
www.nps.gov/hafe/index.htm
Harpers Ferry was the site of John Brown's raid (1859) and the largest surrender of Union troops during the war (1862).

Wisconsin

Civil War Museum of the Upper Middle West
5400 1st Avenue
Kenosha, Wisconsin 53140
www.kenosha.org/civilwar/
Explores life on the home front in Wisconsin, Indiana, Michigan, Illinois, Iowa and Minnesota during the Civil War.

Suggested Reading

Tens of thousands of books have been published on the Civil War, and deciding what to read can be a daunting task—especially if you are new to the subject area. Below is a select reading list on Union-related and general titles to help you get started.

General Histories

Foote, Shelby, *The Civil War: A Narrative*, 3 vols. (1958-1974).

McPherson, James, *Battle Cry of Freedom: The Civil War Era* (1988).

Johnson, Robert U. and Clarence C. Buel, eds., *Battles and Leaders of the Civil War*, 4 vols. (1884-1887).

Coggins, Jack, *Arms and Equipment of the Civil War* (1962).

Soldiers and Soldiering

Beaudot, William J. K., and Herdegen, Lance J., *An Irishman in the Iron Brigade: The Civil War Memoirs of James P. Sullivan, Sergt., Company K, 6th Wisconsin Volunteers* (1993).

Buell, Augustus, *The Cannoneer; Recollections of Service in the Army of the Potomac*. Washington, D.C. (1897).

Burton, William L., *Melting Pot Soldiers: The Union's Ethnic Regiments* (1988).

Cheek, Philip, and Mair Pointon, *History of the Sauk County Riflemen, Known as Company "A" Sixth Wisconsin Veteran Volunteer Infantry, 1861-1865* (1909).

Desjardin, Thomas A., *Stand Firm Ye Boys from Maine: The 20th Maine and the Gettysburg Campaign* (2001).

Dunn, Craig L., *Iron Men, Iron Will: The Nineteenth Indiana Regiment of the Iron Brigade* (1995).

Gaff, Alan D., *On Many a Bloody Field: Four Years in the Iron Brigade* (1997).

Gavin, William Gilfillan, *Campaigning-1865 with the Roundheads: The History of the Hundredth Pennsylvania Veteran Volunteer Infantry Regiment in the American Civil War, 1861-1865* (1989).

Glatthaar, Joseph T., *The March to the Sea and Beyond: Sherman's Troops in the Savannah and Carolina Campaigns* (1985).

Hamblen, Charles P., *Connecticut Yankees at Gettysburg* (1993).

Herdegen, Lance J., and Sharon Murphy, *Four Years With the Iron Brigade: The Civil War Journal of William Ray, Seventh Wisconsin* (2001).

Herdegen, Lance J., *The Iron Brigade in Civil War and Memory: The Black Hats from Bull Run to Appomattox and Thereafter* (2012).

Hess, Earl J., *The Union Soldier in Battle: Enduring the Ordeal of Combat* (1997).

Linderman, Gerald F., *Embattled Courage: The Experience of Combat in the American Civil War* (1987).

Lord, Francis A., *They Fought for the Union* (1860).

McCarter, William, Kevin O'Brien, ed., *My Life in the Irish Brigade* (1997).

McPherson, James M., *For Cause and Comrades: Why Men Fought in the Civil War* (1997).

Mitchell, Reid, *Civil War Soldiers: The Expectations and Their Experiences* (1988).

Moe, Richard, *The Last Full Measure: The Life and Death of the First Minnesota Volunteers* (1993).

Mundy, James H., *Second to None: The Story of the 2nd Maine Volunteers, "The Bangor Regiment"* (1993).

Naiswald, L. Van Loan, *Grape and Canister: The Story of the Field Artillery of the Army of the Potomac, 1861-1865* (1960).

Nolan, Alan T., *The Iron Brigade* (1961).

Pullen, John J., *The Twentieth Maine: A Volunteer Regiment in the Civil War* (1957).

Rowell, John W., *Through the Civil War with Eli Lilly's Indiana Battery* (1975).

Scott, William Forse, *The Story of a Cavalry Regiment: The Career of the Fourth Iowa Veteran Volunteers from Kansas to Georgia 1861-1865* (1893).

Uschan, Michael V., *The Cavalry During the Civil War* (2003).

Wiley, Bell, *The Life of Billy Yank: The Common Soldier of the Union* (1952).

Wilkinson, Warren, *Mother, May You Never See the Sights I Have Seen: The 57th Massachusetts Veteran Volunteers* (1990).

African Americans

Beecham, Robert, Michael E. Stevens, ed., *As If It Were Glory: Robert Beecham's Civil War from the Iron Brigade to the Black Regiments* (1998).

Berlin, Ira, *Freedom's Soldiers: The Black Military Experience in the Civil War* (1998)

Cornish, Dudley Taylor, *The Sable Arm: Negro Troops in the Union Army, 1861-1865* (1966).

Dimcan, Russell, *Where Death and Glory Meet: Robert Could Shaw and the 54th Massachusetts Infantry* (1999).

Glatthaar, Joseph T., *Forged in Battle: The Civil War Alliance of Black Soldiers and White Officers* (1990).

Higginson, Thomas Wentworth, *Army Life in a Black Regiment and Other Writings* (1997).

McPherson, James M., *The Negro's Civil War: How American Blacks Felt and Acted During the War for the Union* (1965).

Women

Berlin, Jean V., and Mary Elizabeth Massey, *Women in the Civil War* (1990).

Garrison, Nancy S., *With Courage and Delicacy: Civil War on the Peninsula, Women and the U.S. Sanitary Commission* (1999).

Silber, Nina, *Daughters of the Union: Northern Women Fight the Civil War* (2005).

Native Americans

Hatch, Thom, *The Blue, the Gray & the Red: Indian Campaigns of the Civil War* (2001).

Hauptman, Laurence M., *A Seneca Indian in the Union Army* (1995).

Hauptman, Laurence M., *Between Two Fires: American Indians in the Civil War* (1995).

Hauptman, Laurence M., *The Iroquois in the Civil War* (1993).

Nichols, David A., *Lincoln and the Indians* (1978).

Fiction

Crane, Stephen, *The Red Badge of Courage* (1895).

Hinman, Wilbur, *Corporal Si Klegg and his Pard* (1887).

Keith, Harold, *Rifles for Waite* (1987).

Pennell, Joseph Stanley, *The History of Rome Hanks and Kindred Matters* (1944).

Shaara, Michael, *Killer Angels* (1974).

Navy

Anderson Bern, *By Sea and by River: The Navy History of the Civil War* (1962).

Davis, William C., *Duel Between the First Ironclads* (1975).

Gosnell, H. Allen, *Guns on the Western Waters: The Story of the River Gunboats in the Civil War* (1949).

Ringle, Dennis, *Life in Mr. Lincoln's Navy* (1998)

Symonds, Craig, *Lincoln and His Admirals* (2008).

Cavalry

Evans, David, *Sherman's Horsemen: Union Cavalry Operations in the Atlanta Campaign* (1999).

Starr, Stephen Z., *The Union Cavalry in the Civil War*, 3 vols. (1979).

Tobie, Edward P., *The History of the First Maine Cavalry 1861-1865* (1987).

Uschan, Michael V., *The Cavalry During the Civil War* (2003).

Genealogy

Groene, Bertram Hawthorne, *Tracing Your Civil War Ancestor* (1989).

INDEX

Lance Herdegen speaking at Camp Randall in Wisconsin in 2012.

About the Author

Award-winning journalist Lance J. Herdegen is the former director of the Institute of Civil War Studies at Carroll University. He previously worked as a reporter and editor for United Press International (UPI) news service covering national politics and civil rights. He currently serves as the historical consultant for the Civil War Museum of the Upper Middle West.

Lance is widely regarded as the world's leading authority on the Iron Brigade. He is the author of many articles, and his books include: *Four Years with the Iron Brigade: The Civil War Journal of William R. Ray, Seventh Wisconsin Volunteers*; *The Men Stood Like Iron: How the Iron Brigade Won its Name*; *In the Bloody Railroad Cut at Gettysburg* (with William Beaudot); *"Those Damned Blackhats!" The Iron Brigade in the Gettysburg Campaign*; and *The Iron Brigade in Civil War and Memory: The Black Hats from Bull Run to Appomattox and Thereafter*.

Lance is currently finishing a book on the Battle of Brawner's Farm (Gainesville), part of the Second Manassas Campaign.